THE ECONOMIC DEVELOPMENT
OF COMMUNIST CHINA
1949–1960

THE ECONOMIC DEVELOPMENT
OF COMMUNIST CHINA
1949–1960

BY

T. J. HUGHES and D. E. T. LUARD

SECOND EDITION

Issued under the auspices of the
Royal Institute of International Affairs

OXFORD UNIVERSITY PRESS
LONDON   NEW YORK   TORONTO

Oxford University Press, Amen House, London E.C.4

GLASGOW NEW YORK TORONTO MELBOURNE WELLINGTON
BOMBAY CALCUTTA MADRAS KARACHI LAHORE DACCA
CAPE TOWN SALISBURY NAIROBI IBADAN ACCRA
KUALA LUMPUR HONG KONG

First edition 1959
Second edition 1961 *and reprinted* 1962

*Printed in Great Britain by
Jarrold & Sons Ltd, Norwich*

CONTENTS

THE PROSPECTS FOR THE FUTURE

PREFACE

THE material on which the following work is based is derived almost entirely from Chinese official sources. The authors have no means of verifying the accuracy of most of this information. Though they have no reason to believe that official statistics are deliberately falsified, they appear sometimes, especially in recent years, to contain a considerable element of wishful thinking. This is especially true of agricultural statistics which cannot always be easily checked by the central authorities. Certainly the figures are usually so presented as to give as favourable a picture as possible of China's economic achievements. The authors have tried, so far as possible, to analyse and assess this presentation; but they must in many cases be content with recording the statements of the Chinese authorities themselves.

No sources are given for most statements of fact. If this had been done almost every sentence would have required a reference. Sources have, however, wherever possible, been given for direct quotations of statements by members of the Chinese Government, and for a few especially significant or controversial statements of fact. In addition, where Chinese official documents, laws, resolutions, and other publications are quoted, the most readily available English-language version of these has if possible been indicated.

The authors wish to express their appreciation to members of the staff of Chatham House, and in particular to Miss Sally Davies (now Mrs. P. J. Mackesy), Miss Jane Godfrey, and Miss Hermia Oliver for the help they have given in the preparation of this volume.

February 1959

ABBREVIATIONS

BBC	BBC, *Summary of World Broadcasts*, Pt. V.
CCP	Chinese Communist Party.
First Five-Year Plan	CCP, *First Five-Year Plan for Development of the National Economy of the People's Republic of China in 1953–1957*. Peking, 1956.
JMJP	*Jenmin Jih Pao* (People's Daily).
KMT	Kuomintang.
NCNA	New China News Agency, London edition.
Proposals for Second Five-Year Plan	*Proposals of the 8th National Party Congress for the Second Five-Year Plan for Development of the National Economy, 1958–1962* (*NCNA*, Suppl. No. 249, 4 October 1956).
..	Not available.

THE FIRST TASKS
OF THE NEW GOVERNMENT

I

CHINA'S TRADITIONAL ECONOMY

CHINA has traditionally been regarded as consisting of two parts, China Proper, composed of the eighteen provinces within the Great Wall; and Outer China, consisting of the former dependencies beyond the Wall, Manchuria, Mongolia, Sinkiang, and Tibet. The Great Wall marked the line between the agricultural civilization of historical China and the mainly pastoral and nomadic communities beyond, which were only comparatively recently conquered. China 'within the Wall' was not much more than one-third of the total area of the country; but it contained about 95 per cent. of the total population.

The most fertile areas of China are the basins of the great rivers and the east coast. Agriculture and population have therefore concentrated in these districts; and the principal waterways, the Yellow, the Huai, the Yangtze, and the Pearl Rivers, flowing out of the mountains in the west to the eastern sea-board, have largely patterned the economic life of the country, dividing it into the three distinct regions—North China, Central China, and South China—of China Proper. Among these there is a considerable range of climate, from the continental-type weather of the north, through the temperate zone of Central China with its mild winters and hot moist summers, to the perpetual humid heat of the south. There is also a good deal of variety in geographical formation. The north and east of the country are mainly flat and fairly low-lying, while the west and south-west are mountainous. Most of the country has a monsoon climate, with winds blowing from the north-west in the winter and off the sea in the summer.

The Agricultural Economy

China has always been a predominantly agricultural community. The normal pattern (which has not yet been much altered) was that about three-quarters of the population were directly engaged in agricultural work, while even more, probably about four-fifths, were dependent on the land. But a very large proportion of the country was generally considered uncultivable (nearly 90 per cent. of the area of Greater China, and about 70 per cent. of China Proper) and the amount of potentially fertile land still not brought into cultivation was small. The proportion actually in use was estimated in the 1930's as 27 per cent. of the area of China Proper, or 240–250 million acres.[1]

As a result a marked concentration of population developed in the alluvial plains and river basins, in the North China plain, the Huai valley, the Yangtze delta, the central Yangtze basin, and the Pearl basin. Chinese farming bore a close resemblance to market-gardening, with the fields divided into tiny holdings, looking more like strips of garden than farms. The constant population pressure, and the perpetual subdivision of the land through the centuries as a result of Chinese rules of inheritance, had by the 1930's produced an average farm of about 3·31 acres, compared with one of 39·74 acres in Denmark, 77·3 acres in England and Wales, and 156·85 acres in the United States.[2] However, the soil of China, after some thousands of years of cultivation, has, through the intensive use of natural fertilizers, still retained much of its fertility; though in some areas the denudation of vegetation, taken for fuel, fodder, and fertilizer, has produced serious problems of erosion.

Differences of climate dictated a variety of crops and rural economies in the different regions. The main crop division is between the wheat belt of the north and the rice zone of the south, though both crops are raised to some extent all over the country. The north is the area of 'dry' produce such as wheat, millet, kaoliang (sorghum), and maize, with wheat as the most common. In the south there are 'wet' crops, and double or treble cropping, with rice the main product in the river basins. Between these two major regions there is a transitional zone, but there is a fairly definite line of division running just north of the Yangtze. In 1937 about 45 per cent. of the cultivated land was estimated as under wheat, and about the same under rice.

Among leguminous crops soya beans are the most important.

[1] J. L. Buck, *Land Utilization in China* (University of Nanking, 1937).
[2] Ibid., pp. 267–8.

This is a food resource of great versatility, which can be used for human and animal food, for oil, or for manufacturing purposes, and has recently become one of China's chief exports. Other food crops are peanuts, cultivated chiefly for their oil, sweet potatoes, and other vegetables.

Thus the main Chinese crops are those directly usable for human consumption, particularly grains, beans, and vegetables. Pressure of population has made it necessary to produce the greatest amount of food possible per unit of land. But despite the high intensity of labour, yields were low; the average pre-war yield of wheat was 9·7 quintals per hectare compared with 21·2 in Britain and 33·1 in Denmark, and even rice yields were significantly lower than in Japan, though higher than in India.[1] As a result the country has not always been self-supporting in essential foodstuffs. During the first fifty years of this century China was a net importer of rice, though the amount was not large in relation to the total amount consumed. But there was a gradual progress towards self-sufficiency in the period up to 1937.

There is also quite an important production of commercial crops. These are partly used domestically and partly sold for cash. The chief of them are cotton, silk, tobacco, tung-oil, and tea. In 1936 China was among the world's largest cotton producers, her total output being about 8·5 million quintals of ginned cotton, or nearly one-eighth of the world supply. By that time the country was practically self-sufficient in raw cotton, and imported only a few specialities.

Within the limitations of his resources the Chinese farmer was skilful, though he was conservative in his methods and many of his implements were primitive—wooden ploughs are still common in many parts of China. In 1946 nearly 90 per cent. of the farm area was under crops, compared with 27 per cent. in England and 12 per cent. in the United States. This difference reflects an important contrast between Chinese and Western agriculture. In China, because of the low rainfall during the winter months and the intense pressure on the land, there is little pasture in most areas. Resources are used most economically in growing directly consumable crops, and animal

[1] Buck, *Chinese Farm Economy*, p. 208.

husbandry is not practised to any great extent except in the North West. Meat is thus something of a luxury in China. Animals, such as oxen and water-buffaloes, if owned at all,[1] are reared for draught purposes rather than for consumption. But poultry and pigs are quite commonly kept—eggs, for example, are quite an important item among Chinese exports.

The control of the rivers was a factor of vital importance within this economy. Made necessary by the perpetual disasters from drought and flood, it took the form of an elaborate system of canals and an extensive network of dykes along the main waterways, though these have not prevented the continued and frequent recurrence of such calamities. The canals also served as an important means of transport. But communications as a whole were nearly always poor, with the result that some parts of the country were often virtually cut off from others, while in many areas the control of the central Government was frequently tenuous or even non-existent.

Over the centuries a great growth of population took place. Although there is an element of speculation in Chinese population estimates, it seems probable that, as a result of a long period of internal peace, the introduction of new crops, and an expansion of the cultivated area, the population approximately doubled between the seventeenth and nineteenth centuries. In the middle of the nineteenth century it was estimated at about 340 million, and by the 1930's rose to a figure of perhaps 450–500 million.

According to the latest census taken in 1953 the population of mainland China was then about 582 million. It is thought now to be rising at a rate of about 12–15 million a year. The town population has been estimated as about 20–25 per cent. of the whole, of whom nearly half live in towns of under 10,000 inhabitants. Pressure of population on the land has been intense, resulting, according to figures given by the Nationalist Government in 1946, in an average division of cultivable area per member of the farm population of about two-thirds of an acre, compared with 8·1 acres in the United States. But this figure was probably based on the old estimates of China's population,

[1] According to Buck, in the inter-war period only 34·1 per cent. of all farms had oxen, 18 per cent. buffaloes, 18 per cent. donkeys, 6 per cent. mules, and 5 per cent. horses (*Chinese Farm Economy*, p. 231).

and more recent estimates suggest that the present average may be only about half an acre.

Investigations carried out in rural China in the 1930's showed that, for the country as a whole, about 50 per cent. of the farmers were owners of the land they worked, just under 33 per cent. were part-owners, and about 17 per cent. were tenants.[1] There was, however, a good deal of regional variation, and tenancy was much more widespread in South China than in North China. It was estimated that about 75 per cent. of the farmers in the northern wheat region were peasant-proprietors, while, in the southern rice region, under 40 per cent. were owners, 25 per cent. were tenant farmers, and over 35 per cent. were part-owners. There were also some areas where all the farmers were owners and others where they were all tenants. The pattern was for tenancy to increase, especially in areas near the Yangtze, and to be the rule in Hunan, Kiangsi, Szechwan, and Kwangtung. In some parts of the country tenants of long standing were considered to have acquired 'surface rights'. Rents, which were normally collected in kind, were extremely high, often as much as 50 per cent. and sometimes even 70 per cent. of the main crop.

Much fragmentation of farms had come about. An average farm had just over 3 acres and was divided into five or six separate strips, with a distance of nearly half a mile between farmhouse and strip. But these averages hid very considerable inequalities in the size of farms: 36 per cent. of the farms were under 1·7 acres and 25 per cent. were between 1·7 and 3·4. And there was considerable regional variation, the largest farms being found in the north-western provinces.

China's Resources

According to surveys initiated by the Chinese Geological Survey in the 1920's, China possessed adequate physical resources for 'a very considerable industrial development' in support of agriculture, but not for industrialization on the scale of modern, highly industrialized countries. The present Government claim, however, to have made important discoveries since that time (and in view of the inadequacy of the prospecting previously

[1] Buck, *Land Utilization in China*, p. 9.

undertaken this is by no means unlikely), and declare that China has ample resources to become an important industrial power.

China has much greater coal resources than any other country in Asia. They are probably inferior only to those of the Soviet Union and the United States. The reserves of China Proper were estimated at about 440,000 million metric tons by the Nationalist authorities in 1947, and there is probably a further 20,000 million tons in Manchuria. Nearly one-fifth was thought to be anthracite, most of the rest being bituminous. The present Government have since claimed 'potential reserves' about three times as big as this, and actual workable deposits of nearly 50,000 million tons. But an essential for modern industrial development is a high proportion of coking coal, and the Chinese were not formerly believed to have very large reserves of this. In 1936 the Chinese coal mines had an output of about 22 million tons.

Oil resources have not been fully explored, but are not thought to be extensive. There have long been known to be oil shales in Manchuria, the most important of which were previously those at Fushun. But many more are now said to have been discovered, including one gigantic field at Pei An in Manchuria. The main reserves of oil previously known, however, were those at Yumen in Kansu, which still provide the greater part of current Chinese production. The present Government are now beginning to exploit new deposits in the Tzungaria basin in north Sinkiang, which it is hoped will provide half of the total Chinese production by 1962. They also claim to have discovered important deposits in the Tsaidam basin in Chinghai, in the Kiuchuan basin in Kansu, in central Szechwan, and on the borders of Inner Mongolia. These deposits are said to have an annual capacity of more than 100 million tons. Such estimates are considered by many to be optimistic; even so, the figure represents less than a third of annual production in the United States. And the fact that oil production was the one important sphere in which the targets of the first Five-Year Plan were not reached, and the recent emphasis in official statements on the development of synthetic supplies, may indicate that, even with recent discoveries, natural oil resources are not plentiful.

Previous estimates of iron-ore resources varied between 1,200 million and 2,700 million tons. The present Chinese Government, however, on the basis of recent prospecting, have for some time claimed deposits of more than 12,000 million metric tons.[1] Nearly three-quarters of the deposits known previously were in Manchuria, though the metal content of these was low (under 40 per cent.). The new deposits are said to have been found in Manchuria, the Kilian mountains in the North West, Szechwan, Hainan, and east Kwangtung. The Chinese Geological Survey before the war considered the reserves then known as probably sufficient for China's own industrial needs for a long time to come, presumably in the light of such industrialization as was then contemplated; and if the recent claims are borne out, China should certainly have enough iron to meet her needs within the foreseeable future, even on present plans for industrialization. In 1936, total output of iron ore was only just over 2 million tons, mainly from Manchuria; and the country was largely dependent on foreign supplies of iron and steel.

China's strongest resource position is in the field of non-ferrous metals, such as tin, lead, molybdenum, and particularly in tungsten and antimony. All of these are found in considerable quantities in the mountainous regions of the south-west.[2]

The chief mineral resources needed for industrialization on any considerable scale are, it is generally agreed, coal, petroleum, iron, and copper. While there seem to be good or adequate supplies of coal, iron, and most of the non-ferrous metals in China, there are probably not, so far as can at present be judged, any very great reserves of petroleum or copper. If these deficiencies are confirmed, China may be obliged to depend on imports of those commodities in undertaking any programme of large-scale industrialization.

China's Traditional Industries

China has known no large-scale industry until the last fifty years. None of her traditional industries were normally organized

[1] The most recent claims, which are almost certainly greatly inflated, are very much larger (see p. 71 below).

[2] The Government have recently claimed that the Chinese deposits of tungsten, tin, and molybdenum are the largest in the world, the deposits of iron ore, manganese, lead, and aluminium the second largest, and those of coal the third largest (*NCNA*, 8 Jan., 10 Feb., and 29 Dec. 1958).

in units so large as those known during the Roman Empire or in medieval Europe. Many were carried on by individual craftsmen who, having served an apprenticeship, maintained one-man businesses, sometimes with the help of apprentices or of members of their families. At the same time many goods which in Europe were made by specialist craftsmen or in workshops, such as clothes, furniture, and other household objects, were often made in China by the individual peasant within the home.

The largest-scale industry was probably salt mining, which at various times in Chinese history was nationalized and run by the state. (The first controversies in China about the relative merits of state control and private enterprise date back to the second century B.C.) There were also tin, iron, and coal mines, though none of these commodities were used to the extent that they have been in Europe. Gold, silver, and copper were mined for use in currency and ornaments.

For the rest the principal industries were mainly those devoted to the production of luxury goods, designed largely for the use of the imperial court and a comparatively small wealthy class. The most flourishing of these were the porcelain and brocade industries, but there was also significant production of enamel-ware, lacquer, ivory, and jade-ware, as well as of other ornaments. These craft industries were normally organized into guilds not unlike those which existed in medieval Europe.

Finally there were the cottage industries, often carried on by the peasants' womenfolk or the peasants themselves in their off-seasons, of sericulture, basket-work, weaving, embroidery, and pottery. The products of these obtained a wider distribution than those of the luxury industries and might sometimes be bought by at least the better off among the villagers themselves and townspeople.

Finance

Under the empire revenue was principally obtained from two sources, direct taxation on the individual landholder, originally a form of tribute and often collected in kind, and the salt gabelle. Taxation was collected by officials who during recent times might farm out the right of collection to local landowners or money-lenders. The incidence of this taxation, over and above what was necessary to cover the figure for which the local official was responsible to the central Government, depended on the relative ruthlessness or moderation of whoever collected it. Since there was no distinction made between the personal and official funds of local officials there was little incentive to moderation (other than the exhortations of Confucian doctrine). There was also in later years a tax on the internal movement of commodities. Income-tax was unknown. Expenditure was devoted primarily to the upkeep of the imperial court, including the central administration and the maintenance of the armed forces.

Money was very little used in the peasant economy. Until the last few years it has been quite normal for a peasant household to have a money income of only a few pounds a year. Money-lenders existed, charging anything up to 10 per cent. a month interest, but there were no Western-type banks or any large-scale financial institutions.

Modern Industry

Until very recent times the development of modern industry, mining, and railway construction in China was chiefly financed by Western and Japanese capital. The Treaty of Nanking of 1842 opened China to Western trade, and the growth of foreign settlements or concessions had an important influence on subsequent economic development. For the first time the methods of large-scale commercial organizations and modern financial institutions were introduced into China. Under the Treaty of Shimonoseki of 1895 China agreed to open additional ports and to permit foreign industrial enterprise at the ports.

As a result a number of foreign-owned cotton mills and other factories were introduced into the country, mainly in Shanghai. A scanty network of railways linking the main parts of China Proper began to be built, largely financed by foreign capital. But the most important railway systems were built by the Russians in North Manchuria and by the Japanese in South Manchuria.

The revolution of 1911 left the country in chaos. There was no effective central authority to direct economic policy, and foreign investment became extremely hazardous. As a result development came almost to a standstill. Even after the assumption of power by Chiang Kai-shek in 1926–30, the situation was not very much better. The Nationalist Government at no time possessed undisputed control of the whole of China Proper, let alone the outlying provinces. Parts of the country were under the effective control of local war-lords. In some areas the Government's authority was resisted from the start of the régime by the Communists. The Government were never powerful enough to enforce their will against the Western powers, who still possessed independent settlements, extra-territorial rights, concessions, leases, and other important privileges. In 1931, only a year after Chiang Kai-shek obtained control of Peking, the Japanese, by taking possession of Manchuria, began the series of infiltrations that was to culminate in 1937 in the outbreak of full-scale war between the two countries. And within a year of the end of that war the régime was, once again, engaged in civil war against the Communists.

These conditions were not propitious to rapid economic development. Foreign investment was not encouraged, either by the internal disorder or by the chauvinistic tone of the Government's public pronouncements of policy. Native private investment was limited, partly by the lack of a well-organized capital market, partly by the exorbitant cost of borrowing and the competition in many fields of well-established foreign firms (whose position was at first facilitated by foreign control of tariffs), but mainly by the desperately low level of the national income, which, as in other underdeveloped countries, made any worth-while rate of capital formation almost impossible through private channels alone. At the same time the lack of effective control over the country, the inexperience and later the corruption of government administrators, and the primitive state of the country's fiscal system also prevented any effective action to promote economic development on the part of the Government.

The system of taxation was improved but remained totally inadequate to the country's needs. About 90 per cent. of the revenue came from indirect taxes, of which nearly one-third derived from customs duties, and about another third from the salt tax. In addition there were multitudinous, complex, and arbitrarily imposed local taxes. Income-tax was not introduced until the beginning of the war against Japan.

With very few exceptions the budgets introduced by the régime were deficit-financed. In many cases revenue was less than 80 per cent. of expenditure, and the Government were obliged to resort to extensive borrowing at a high rate of interest. A substantial part of the budget was devoted to the debt services. Specific taxes and part of the customs revenue were pledged as security against these borrowings.

Nor was the Government's revenue employed for any very useful economic purpose. A large proportion was absorbed by military expenditure, first for the campaign against the Communists and later for the Japanese War. No large-scale public works, for example in the field of irrigation or agricultural development, were undertaken. As a result of the extensive government borrowing and the increasing use of currency, together with the lack of any substantial increase in productive resources, inflation was recurrent, especially towards the end of the régime's existence, and three successive currencies collapsed during its period of office.

In origin the Government were socialistic in their aims, in conformity with Sun Yat-sen's writings, but as time progressed they came increasingly into alliance with business interests. In the early years grandiose schemes of economic development were drawn up, though never implemented. In 1931 a National Economic Council was formed, but, beyond giving some technical assistance in isolated fields, this does not seem to have played any very effective part in promoting economic development. During the war an increasing number of factories in Chinese-held territory were run and owned by the state. At the end of the war, all enterprises formerly owned by the Japanese and by Chinese collaborators in China Proper and in Manchuria were taken over by the Government, although it was intended that they should eventually be sold to private enterprises. By this time, however, many of the leading Nationalist officials had extensive business interests or connexions, and the party came increasingly to rely on the support of the capitalist classes. Widespread corruption, and the priority almost universally accorded to family obligations above all others, rendered government intervention largely ineffective in promoting economic development.

At the same time, in conformity with public opinion among educated Chinese at this period, the Government were intensely nationalistic in their aims. While never militarily powerful enough to enforce their views against the Western powers in matters of major importance, they managed to obtain from them some concessions. In 1929–30 control over tariffs was restored to the Chinese Government. Some concessions and leases were given up. But the most important foreign privileges, the foreign settlements and extra-territorial rights, were not abandoned by the major Western powers until towards the end of the war.

With the restoration of tariff autonomy there was a rise in import duties, especially on manufactures. Under this protection there was an expansion of native-controlled, as well as foreign, manufacturing industry. There was a growth also in the number of Chinese-owned businesses as well as of native-controlled banks and other institutions. This development was directly encouraged by the Government, both by attempts to impose special taxes and other disabilities on foreign firms, and by the stipulation that a given proportion of shareholdings and directorships should be in Chinese hands. Chinese consumers were encouraged to patronize native businesses. Perhaps fortunately for the development of the Chinese economy foreign business activity was not too seriously inhibited.

Despite all the difficulties some progress was made. By 1937 there were about 7,000 miles of railways in China Proper, air lines linked the major cities, and highway mileage had expanded from 20,000 in 1927 to 75,000 in 1937. In Shanghai, Tientsin, Hankow, and a few other centres there was a fairly rapid expansion of modern, often foreign-owned, businesses. Employment in industry rose to over a million, while about 10 million more were engaged in handicrafts.[1] In the countryside improved facilities for credit were provided.

But the most spectacular economic development on Chinese soil was made by the Japanese in Formosa and especially in

[1] Ou Pao-san and Wang Foh-shen, 'Production and Employment in Pre-War China', *Economic Journal*, Sept. 1946.

Manchuria, where they developed a flourishing heavy-industry complex. In 1937 about half the coal, about two-thirds of the iron, and something like nine-tenths of the steel produced in China came from Manchuria. In China Proper such modern industry as had developed was almost entirely light industry, especially textiles, which accounted for nearly half the total industrial output. There was almost no heavy industry.[1] The total output of steel outside Manchuria was only 50,000 tons, of pig-iron 430,000 tons, of coal 20 million tons, and of electricity 2,500 million kwh.[2]

A large part of the modern industry of the country was foreign-owned. Even for light industrial goods the country was dependent on imports for between 50 and 70 per cent. of requirements, and industry was largely concentrated in the Treaty Ports and along the Yangtze valley. Shanghai accounted for about half the industrial output. Capital was scarce and expensive. There was no organized security market, and virtually no public issues of industrial securities. What Chinese businesses existed were mainly run as personal and family concerns.

At the end of the war this position was not substantially altered. Though massive economic assistance was provided, both by UNRRA and directly by the United States, little of this was put to effective economic use, largely as a result of the corruption of Nationalist officials. The Nationalist Government never obtained effective control of the country's most important centre of heavy industry built up by the Japanese in Manchuria. These installations were almost completely dismantled and removed to the Soviet Union at the time of the Russian occupation of the area in 1945–6. From 1946 onwards Nationalist control of the region was disputed by the Communists and their Manchurian allies. Over the next three years the energies of the Government were too preoccupied with the struggle against the Communists for them to give any effective attention to economic problems.

[1] In 1937 only about 9 per cent. of the industrial resources of China Proper could be classified as capital industry, including communications, construction, water and electricity supply, stone and brick works, metallurgy, &c. (*A China Manual*, a Chinese Government Information Handbook, 1944, p. 126.)

[2] Ibid., p. 127.

When the Communists came to power in 1949, by far the greater part of the country carried on, as for the last 2,000 years, an early-iron-age economy. Agricultural techniques were backward and yields low. The greater part of industry consisted of handicrafts. A sprinkling of modern industry had developed, mainly in the ports of the eastern sea-board. A small, efficient, but now largely plundered nucleus of heavy industry had grown up in Manchuria. The main task of industrial development in China had barely begun.

II

THE ECONOMIC OBJECTIVES
OF THE CHINESE COMMUNIST PARTY

THE Chinese Communist Party (CCP) was, from its origin, a fully Marxist party. It was founded by a group on whom, as on many others of their generation in China, the Russian Revolution had exerted a profound impact, and who saw in the path followed by Russia the cure for the backwardness and humiliating impotence of China in face of the West, of which educated Chinese were at that time becoming acutely aware. The declared aim of the Party since the very beginning, therefore, has been the establishment of a fully socialist society in China, in which all the means of production and distribution should be in the hands of the state. The manifesto issued at the second Congress of the Party in 1922 declared that its aims were to struggle for 'the dictatorship of the workers and peasants, the abolition of private property, and the gradual attainment of a communist society'.

From soon after its foundation, however, the Party was in alliance with the nascent Kuomintang (KMT), which the Soviet Union saw as the chief hope for a successful revolutionary movement in China. Thus the CCP had to renounce, at least in public, any immediate aspirations towards bringing about a radical transformation of the Chinese economy. In the joint manifesto[1] issued by Sun Yat-sen and A. A. Joffe, the Soviet emissary to the KMT, in January 1923, it was stated:

Dr. Sun is of the opinion that, because of the non-existence of conditions favourable to their successful application in China, it is not possible to carry out either communism or even the Soviet system [i.e. the system prevailing in the Soviet Union at that time, 1923] in China. M. Joffe agrees entirely with this view; he is . . . of the opinion that China's most important, most pressing problem is the completion of national unification and the attainment of national independence.

[1] C. Brandt and others, *A Documentary History of Chinese Communism* (London, Allen & Unwin, 1952), p. 70.

Thus the immediate programmes set out in the manifestos of
the first two or three national congresses of the CCP make no
mention of plans for wide-scale nationalization or indeed any
other measures much affecting the Chinese economy other than
reforms in agriculture. Their demands concentrated on calls for
reduction in taxation and for tenancy reform.

After the break-up of the alliance with the KMT in 1927, the
CCP had no hold over, nor even any widespread membership
in, any industrial area, and their activities were for the most
part concentrated in a few scattered agricultural regions over
which they retained military control. Questions of industrial
policy therefore became increasingly academic.

The principal area held from 1927 to 1934 was a region in
Kiangsi, declared a Soviet Republic in 1931. The policies of the
Communist authorities were almost exclusively concerned with
the agricultural problems of the area, and in particular with the
carrying out of land reform, though tax reforms were also introduced and usury abolished. In theory under the constitution of
the Republic it was said to be the purpose of the régime to
'restrict the development of capitalism with a view to liberating
the toiling masses from capitalist exploitation and leading them
to the socialist order of society'. But this had little meaning,
since the Communists at that time were leading a guerrilla
existence in the hills and rural districts of the region, and held
no industrial area where such policies might be put into effect.

After the long march to Shensi in North China, the Chinese
Communists were still almost entirely confined to rural districts.
Here, however, they had time to establish themselves and,
with the beginning of the Japanese War, began to enjoy
some respite from the continual harassing of the Nationalist
armies which had restricted their activities in Kiangsi. Small-
scale industry began to develop. In particular, since the Chinese
Nationalists allowed no arms to reach the Communist armies
from sources under their control, small munitions workshops
were set up to supplement the supply of arms captured from the
Japanese. There were also coal, iron, and salt mines; small
factories for such articles as paper, soap, shoes, buttons, and
batteries; an oilfield and an iron foundry—all primitive and on
a very small scale. Many of these were run by the army with

soldiers as workers. For the most part the enterprises were nationalized and run by the state. There was state trading on a wide scale. But co-operatives were also encouraged in which the soldiers were allowed to participate and invest their earnings. There were also some private undertakings, though these were nearly all working on government orders. In agriculture there was redistribution of land and the peasants were encouraged to develop mutual-aid groups.

A future economic programme for the Party was set out in Mao Tse-tung's *On New Democracy* published in 1940. The book described a two-stage revolution. In the first stage, called 'new democracy', a united front of all popular classes would be formed under Communist Party leadership, directed against 'imperialism, feudalism, and bureaucratic capitalism'.[1] Following the stage of 'new democracy' there was to be a second revolution, achieved without violence, when a 'classless socialist society' would be created. But the second revolution would need considerable preparation and, in the meanwhile, the economic conditions for this transformation, the development of industry and agriculture, must be prepared.

In the economy of the 'new democracy' the state-operated enterprises, 'under the leadership of the proletariat' were to 'constitute the leading force in the economy'. They would be the spearhead for the gradual socialization of the entire economy. Land would be confiscated from landlords and distributed to the peasants, although rich peasants would continue to be tolerated. This was the policy of 'equalization of land-ownership', which was said to put into practice Sun Yat-sen's famous slogan, 'land to the tillers'.

China's economy was to be developed by the application of the policies of 'control of capital' and 'equalization of land-ownership'. But the People's Republic would not, at the first stage, take over capitalist private property as such, or forbid capitalist production, so long as the people were not being exploited. This programme remained the official policy of the

[1] After they came to power, the Chinese Communist Party did in fact preserve the appearance of a 'united front' when undertaking the political reorganization of the country; this was embodied in the Chinese People's Political Consultative Conference, which included representatives of the 'minority parties' and 'non-party delegates'.

Party right up to the time of its assumption of power in 1949.

The Common Programme[1] adopted by the Chinese People's Political Consultative Conference in September 1949 embodied some of the theories of 'new democracy'. Article 26 laid down the policy of the Central People's Government on the relationship between the public and private sectors of the economy:

The State shall co-ordinate and regulate the state-owned economy, co-operative economy, individual economy of peasants and handicraftsmen, private capitalist economy and State capitalist economy[2] in the spheres of operation, supply of raw materials, markets, labour, technical equipment, policies of public finance and trade, etc., so that all components of the social economy can play their part and effect division of work and co-operate under the leadership of the state-owned economy to promote the development of the entire social economy.

China, therefore, was to be a 'mixed economy', divided into the five sectors of state-owned economy, co-operative economy, the individual economy of peasants and handicraftsmen, the private capitalist economy, and the state capitalist economy. Private enterprise was to be allowed and encouraged in the interests of production, but would be subject to government control. It was stated that 'State-owned trading organs shall undertake to adjust supply and demand, stabilize commodity prices and foster the people's co-operatives'. The Government, therefore, were to have the overall responsibility of working out suitable price policies in accordance with economic conditions and maintaining an appropriate difference between wholesale and retail prices and between prices in different areas.

Article 33 of the Common Programme outlined the Government's plans for economic planning. This said:

The Central People's Government shall as early as possible draw up a general plan for rehabilitating and developing the main branches of the public and private economy of the entire country, determine the division of work and co-operation between the Central and local Governments in economic construction and carry out unified co-ordination of the mutual relations between the economic departments of the Central and local governments.

[1] *NCNA*, Spec. Suppl. No. 29, 29 Sept. 1949.
[2] In the state capitalist economy, capital is privately supplied and interest paid on it, while direction and control are mainly in the hands of the state.

During the first years of their rule, the Communist leaders declared in their speeches that their aim was the creation of a powerful modern industry with which China might be built into a great power. In a speech to the National People's Congress in September 1954 Chou En-lai said that the fundamental objectives of the Chinese Revolution were to release the productive forces of the country from the oppression of imperialism, feudalism, and bureaucratic capitalism, from the yoke of capitalism, and from the restriction of small-scale production, so that the national economy could develop systematically and rapidly along the road to socialism, the material and cultural life of the people could be raised, and the independence and security of the country could be strengthened. But the new industrial economy was to be socially-owned. The 'General Line of the State' introduced in 1952, after the task of reconstruction was said to be completed, provided for the completion of 'socialist transformation', i.e. the nationalization of the entire economy, including agriculture, within the course of three Five-Year Plans.

The constitution of the People's Republic,[1] adopted by the National People's Congress on 20 September 1954, outlines the aims which had by that time come to guide the economic policies of the Government. Thus the preamble states:

From the founding of the People's Republic of China to the attainment of a socialist society is a period of transition. During the transition the fundamental task of the state is, step by step, to bring about the socialist industrialisation of the country, and, step by step, to accomplish the socialist transformation of agriculture, handicrafts and capitalist industry and commerce.

In Articles 4 to 7 the different sectors of the economy are identified and described. The .state sector, a socialist sector 'owned by the whole people', is 'the leading force in the national economy and the material basis for the socialist reconstruction carried out by the state'. The co-operative sector is 'either socialist economy collectively owned by the working masses, or semi-socialist economy in part collectively owned by the working masses'. Partial collective ownership is considered as a transitional form by means of which individual peasants,

[1] *NCNA*, Suppl. No. 219, 20 Oct. 1954.

individual handicraftsmen, and other individual working people organize themselves in 'their advance towards collective ownership by the working masses'. The other forms of ownership corresponding to the remaining sectors of the economy are ownership by 'individual working people' and 'capitalist ownership'.

Transitional forms to be used in the socialist transformation of agriculture and of private industry and commerce were also specified in the constitution, which confirmed policies towards those sectors which had already been evolving since the régime came to power. The chief transitional form for agriculture and handicrafts was the co-operative based on 'the partial collective ownership of the working masses'; for example, the semi-socialist 'agricultural producers' co-operative'. For private industry and commerce the transitional form was the joint state-private enterprise, a form of state capitalism, envisaged as a stage on the road towards complete state ownership.

Nearly all the published programmes of the CCP, especially in the years before it attained power, were formulated not merely as statements of intentions but with a political purpose, that is in order to attract a substantial body of support among the Chinese people, or at least to avoid alienating those who might be frightened by a more extreme platform. It is thus impossible to say how far these programmes corresponded with the Communist leaders' true intentions at any period. The leaders themselves never made any secret of their faith in the doctrines of orthodox Communism, or that their final intention was to create a fully socialist society in China. But in general they avoided committing themselves on the exact means to be employed in bringing this about; and in the meantime they were careful to emphasize those elements of their policy that were likely to win them sympathy among the Chinese population. When they did finally find themselves in control of China, their power was such that they were able to base their policies on their own ideological convictions rather than on popular wishes. And although they have, with characteristic Chinese pragmatism, shown themselves more ready than most other Communist Governments to modify their policies in the light of events, their programme has in general represented an orthodox application of traditional Communist creeds.

III

THE PERIOD OF
ECONOMIC REHABILITATION, 1949–52

IN the autumn of 1949 when the Communists, having conquered most of China, established the Chinese People's Republic, the Chinese economy had for the last three years been exposed to the rigours and violence of a bitter civil war. This in turn had been preceded by the protracted campaigns of the war against Japan from 1937 to 1945 and twenty-five years of civil disorder before that. Serious damage had been suffered by industry, agriculture, and transport, and the first task of the new Government was quite simply to restore as quickly as possible the normal processes of economic life.

A new administrative structure was established. The country was divided into six regions, military and economic administrative zones, each made up of several provinces. Under the provinces were the old counties (*hsien*) and, within these, *hsiang*, which were made up of several villages. Administration was performed by local cadres ('*kanpus*'), chosen largely for political reliability, though not necessarily party members. The government structure was paralleled by, and not always easily distinguishable from, a similar network of Communist Party officials supervising both administrative organs and industrial managements. The new cabinet was the State Administrative Council (replaced in 1954 by the State Council) operating mainly through its functional committees. One of these was the Committee for Economic and Financial Affairs, directing economic affairs and controlling the economic ministries of the Government.

The situation which this machinery faced was critical. Communications had been completely disrupted as a result of the fighting. In many parts industry had been brought almost to a standstill. The marketing and procurement agencies for grain had virtually ceased to function. Currency inflation was rampant. In addition, in the second half of 1949, there were serious floods, said to have affected 30 to 40 per cent. of China's arable land. Industrial output in that year, according to Communist figures, was about 56 per cent. and food production 70–75 per cent. of the previous peaks.

The first task in the economic field was to achieve a stable currency. The depreciation and eventual collapse of three successive currencies under the Nationalist régime—the last, introduced in August 1948, had become almost valueless within six weeks—had probably been the most important single cause of the loss of popular support for that Government and its eventual defeat by the Communists. The new régime was, therefore, well aware of the importance of avoiding similar mistakes.

When the Communist Government took over, the only currencies which played an effective part in Chinese economic life were foreign ones, especially the United States and Mexican dollars. There was a general flight from the gold yuan, the Nationalist currency, which circulated in units of billions. Most people aimed to hold their wealth in commodities. Much trade was by barter and even wage payments were often made in kind. Besides the Nationalist currency, foreign currencies, and currencies issued by individual Chinese banks, there were several different Communist currencies issued in different areas at different times. In May 1949 a unified currency, the People's Currency (*Jen Min Piao*), was introduced for all areas under Communist control. Soon afterwards the use of foreign currencies as a normal medium of exchange was banned and dealing in foreign exchange was made a state monopoly.

But the general distrust of all native currencies, together with the dislocation caused by the fighting, the comparative isolation of large producing areas from consuming areas, and the issue of paper money to cover deficits in government finance, continued to produce considerable inflation even in the new Communist currency. Between June and December 1949 the price index of essential commodities in the principal cities increased by something like thirty times.

One of the most important requirements was to secure a freer movement of commodities, to bring food into the cities, and to increase exchanges between the various regions of China, thus eliminating shortages and providing some outlet for purchasing power. One of the chief causes of inflation in the areas controlled by the Nationalist Government in the period of the civil war had been the inadequate communications, causing local scarcities which sent prices spiralling upwards. In order to restore the physical means of communication, the People's Liberation Army was given the work of repairing and bringing back into use the main railway lines (which play a vital part in the modern Chinese economy). Vigorous efforts were made to restore agricultural and consumer-goods production.

In the course of 1949, as new areas were occupied by the army, a network of large monopolistic trading companies was formed. These provided the new régime with an instrument for its anti-inflationary policy. They facilitated price control by furnishing the Government with reserves of rice, cotton, and other key commodities, which could be placed in the market at strategic moments. They mobilized food and raw materials for the cities. And they sold direct to the peasants from the cities.

After October 1949 state trading companies were formed in all the larger towns and cities. The volume of internal exchanges was increased. Manchuria sent timber and grain to North China in return for cement, tobacco, yarn, and cloth; and Wuhan sent tea, tung oil, tobacco, and peanut oil to Shanghai and Tientsin, for coal, yarn, and petrol. The trading companies bought up the output of some factories wholesale and resold them to other companies in other areas. The virtually complete monopoly of the Government in wholesale trade prevented the exploitation of shortages by merchants and speculators. Nor would the state trading organizations pay excessive prices to producers, who were left entirely at the mercy of the state's purchasers. Finally, by the operation of state retail agencies selling at low prices, the retailers' prices were also kept down.

The state trading companies had other important functions. In 1949 and early 1950 most of the country's industrial resources and distribution facilities were still in the hands of private firms. These could not immediately be taken over, yet the authorities were anxious to acquire the maximum possible control over their output. The establishment of state trading companies, whose orders and contracts might be vital to a private company's survival, was a useful method of ensuring a measure of government control over private enterprise.

In the sphere of public finance too, the Government first concentrated their efforts on price stabilization. Direct control of prices, which in China would undoubtedly have fostered a flourishing black market, played only a small part in these efforts. Determined efforts were made, however, to reduce the volume of money in circulation. The currency holdings of government organs, state-operated enterprises, and co-operatives were centralized in the People's Bank from March 1950 onwards. Drastic economies were enforced in the use of currency by all state agencies. Austerity standards of pay for the Government's military, civil, and educational personnel were introduced through the 'public supplies' system, under which the Government provided daily necessities and a limited sum of spending money. There was a large issue of Victory Bonds, the purchase of which was made virtually compulsory. And severe penalties were imposed against hoarding.

The stabilization of wages was made easier by paying workers on the basis of a 'wage-point'. This was a shifting index based on the price of five basic items of consumer expenditure: rice, oil, coal, flour, and cotton cloth. The current value of the wage-point was published in the newspapers every day. Wages were reckoned on the basis of so many wage-points and thus varied, in monetary terms, from week to week. Pressure from workers for wage increases on the grounds of rises in the cost of living was thus allayed. A similar system was used to safeguard the real value of savings and bank deposits.

By these means a decisive influence was exercised on prices in the first year or so of the new régime's existence. At the same time efforts were made to restore China's foreign trade. Statements designed to reassure both native and foreign business men were made. And the steps taken by the Government to reduce banditry in the countryside, and the return of the country as a whole to more settled conditions, made an important contribution to the restoration of stability in the economic sphere.

Despite these efforts there is no doubt that in the period immediately following the Communist victory there was very serious disruption within the economy. Besides the dislocation inevitably associated with civil war and a change of government, the accession of a Communist régime naturally aroused widespread apprehension and uncertainty among the business community. Travellers to Hong Kong reported that industry in Shanghai was stagnant and that many businesses were closing down. There were said to be serious shortages of raw materials. These probably arose not only from the interruption of previous supply channels, but from the inexperience and inflexibility of Communist officials. Quite often business was made difficult if not impossible for many private firms as a result of a policy of deliberate discrimination and ruthless taxation by some local administrations. In some cases businesses were expropriated without warning and without reason. There were reports of business men being forced to unload all their stocks on to the market, even at a loss, to relieve shortages. There was also said to be a severe shortage of food in some areas. Such difficulties were accentuated by the blockade of the South China ports which the Nationalist authorities in Formosa attempted to enforce at this time.

There seems certainly to have been a good deal of unrest during the first months of the new Government's existence. This was probably caused partly by the devastating floods of 1949 as well as by the Government's heavy financial levies and the rigorous political control. Press reports from Western sources in March 1950 said that thousands were starving, shops were closing, and peasants were rioting. Perhaps as a result, there was some relaxation of the Government's policies in the spring of that year. The state trading companies were used to stimulate economic activity by loans and allocations of orders to private concerns. Taxation was reduced. A revival of private trade started, and later in the year the régime was helped by favourable summer and autumn harvests. This effort at stabilization brought the beginning of a period of economic expansion.

As a result the Government were able to begin to devote themselves to the long-term rehabilitation of the battered economy in preparation for the inauguration of the first Five-Year Plan. This was to occupy them for the next three years. It was a time of considerable pressure on China's economic resources. The Chinese intervention in the Korean War in

October 1950, several intense political campaigns at home, the implementation of nation-wide land reform, and an increasing degree of government penetration of industry all had their impact on the economic situation.

Various measures of economic reorganization were introduced. In January 1950 an important reform of the tax system was announced. This rationalized and unified the large variety of different taxes, varying regionally, which had existed before. The principal taxes were to be the agricultural tax and the tax on industrial and commercial enterprises. But there was in addition to be a new sales tax on all commercial transactions and an income-tax on wages and salaries (thus, as before, income-tax affected only a very small proportion of the population). There were other taxes similar to those imposed in Britain and other European countries, such as excise and customs duties, entertainments tax, property tax (i.e. rates) on urban property, death duties, and a tax on unearned income; but these, even taken together, accounted for a very small proportion of the total revenue.

As a result the Chinese authorities were able to announce with pride that the 1950 budget had been balanced. This was certainly a refreshing contrast to most of the budgets of the previous thirty years. It was made possible by a large increase in revenue, chiefly in the form of the profits of state-run enterprises, and especially of the state trading organizations. It appears, however, to have been at least partly a book-keeping success, achieved by including loan income, which Po I-po the Minister of Finance had originally mentioned as being necessary to make up a 'deficit', as above-line revenue.

In March 1950 the Government introduced centralized management and control of the national finances. This was brought about through the 'Decision on the Centralization of Financial and Economic Work' of the State Administrative Council of 3 March 1950. The main aims of this were to centralize control over national revenue and expenditure; to plan on a nation-wide basis the use of materials and resources; and to introduce the unified control of currency. The most important single factor in achieving better central control was the unification of tax collection, which brought about the direct participation of the central Government in a sphere in which their powers had formerly been delegated to the provincial governments. Taxes were to be paid into 'People's Banks' functioning as local branches of the Bank of China, and as agencies for tax collection throughout the country. The Ministry of Finance, jointly with other ministries and organizations concerned, was to determine and generally supervise the system of taxation, the procedure for controlling revenue and expenditure, and the wage structure and size of staffs of government departments and state enterprises. The Ministry of Finance would also be responsible for the compilation of the state budget, would have at its disposal all national revenues, and would have to approve all items of expenditure under the state budget.

The Korean War brought very severe strains on the economy. In the middle of 1950 there was a rush on the part of manufacturers and industrialists in China, as elsewhere, to assure themselves of future supplies of materials by advance purchases, and sometimes to seek speculative profits in the inflated market created by the outbreak of the war. State-run organizations seem to have been quite as guilty in these respects as the private business men. The Government had to set up a special committee for checking the distribution and supply of materials and preventing hoarding or wastage. Such nation-wide economic disturbances were increased by Chinese intervention in the war in October 1950. Inflationary pressures were generated, and the prices of metals, industrial raw materials, and dyestuffs rose sharply.

The Western press reported considerable hardship in China during the winter of 1950–1, including acute famine conditions in Anhwei, Kiangsu, Shantung, and Hopei, and in several districts in the south-west. Millions of government employees were said to be contributing a considerable part of their salaries, already barely adequate to support them, to national famine-relief funds and war savings. The Chinese authorities admitted that two major crops had been affected by floods and drought, but claimed there was an overall food 'surplus'.

Considerable efforts were made by the Government to counter these pressures. There was increased regimentation, both in the economic and political field. More stringent security controls were introduced. There were widespread purges of 'counter-revolutionaries'. To curb inflation the Government relied on high taxation, forced sales of bonds, and rigid methods of trade and exchange control. 'The army donation campaign', an intensive campaign for contributions to buy tanks, aircraft, &c., for the Korean War, brought in a considerable volume of revenue and helped to siphon off some excess purchasing power. In addition the Government seized the opportunity provided by the Korean War to intensify their control over the business sector through the virulent 'Five Antis' campaign.[1]

Despite these efforts, by the middle of 1951 the Korean War was beginning to make a considerable impact on the Chinese economy. This was shown in a cut in expenditure on construction, the imposition of new surtaxes, and a drive for the use of substitute commodities. The curtailment of national subventions to municipal governments was revealed in a decree of the State Administrative Council of 31 March 1951. Early in 1952 directives were sent to all the provinces demanding that the most stringent economy should be practised in that year. Despite these difficulties, living costs were kept fairly stable. As a result of government control of the supply of such basic commodities as grain, cotton cloth, coal briquettes, and peanut oil, the 'daily necessities' index which determined wages showed little variation, though the prices of some manufactures rose.

At the same time the proportion of publicly owned industry within the economy was continually increasing in relation to the private sector. The output of state-owned industrial enterprises, including co-operatives and industries jointly operated by state and private capital, increased from 36·7 per cent. of the nation's total industrial output in 1949 to 61 per cent. in 1952. The volume of wholesale trade handled by state-owned trading enterprises on the domestic market increased from 44·4 per cent. to over 50 per cent. The state owned all the railways, 80 per cent. of heavy industry, 60 per cent. of the shipping, and 50 per cent. of light industry.

On the whole the pressures generated by efforts to mobilize resources, both for the Korean War and for the gathering

[1] See below, pp. 84–85.

industrialization programme, do not seem to have prevented a fair measure of success in the economic rehabilitation of the country. The Government themselves claimed this had been largely achieved by 1952. In his report on the work of the Government delivered at the meeting of the first session of the first National People's Congress on 23 September 1954 Chou En-lai described the first three years of the régime as having seen the unification of China's mainland, the reform of the agrarian system, and the 'rehabilitation of the national economy'.

By the end of 1952 the total value of the output of industry and agriculture was said to show a 77·5 per cent. increase over 1949 (a particularly bad year). According to official figures, production of coal had reached 63 million tons, just above the highest pre-liberation figure, production of power was 7,000 million kwh., of pig-iron nearly 2 million tons, of steel 1,350,000 tons. Total production of food grains was about 164 million tons, probably just above the previous peak. In general the economic position had been stabilized. As a result, the Government apparently considered that the way had been prepared for the initiation of a more comprehensive and rigidly controlled programme of development.

THE FIVE-YEAR PLANS

IV
THE ESTABLISHMENT OF
THE PLANNING MACHINERY

In the early part of 1950 a rudimentary form of planning was initiated. The procedure in this period, as in the Soviet Union before the introduction of full-scale economic planning, was to set annual production targets, apparently arrived at largely by guess-work, for the principal commodities, such as grain, cotton, or coal. Plans for the 1951 production goals for key industries were discussed at the first National Heavy Industry Planning Conference held in Peking in July 1950. Control figures were then formulated by the Ministry of Heavy Industry. Top priorities were given to steel and chemical fertilizer.

The technique of drawing up the target figure seems to have resembled that used in the Soviet Union at a similar stage. The delegates to the Peking conference returned to their own areas and factories to discuss the general findings with local managers and workers, and to consider the specific production job to be done by each unit under the plan. After the details of the next year's production had been worked out locally, revised estimates were returned to the Ministry of Heavy Industry. Once the Ministry had approved the revised figures, a final draft was drawn up for presentation to the State Administrative Council for approval.

Large-scale planning was of course quite new to China. It was considered that the role of planning in the economy should not be over-emphasized at this time, since privately owned enterprises were 'still indispensable' to China. But delegates to the Peking conference were urged to study the experience of the Soviet Union in this field, and the conference considered methods of working the private sector into the planning process through the placing of government orders, the allocation of raw materials and semi-finished products, and the granting of credits.

Whether as part of the policy of increased regimentation associated with the Korean War, or in anticipation of the policy of national economic planning due to be launched in the following year, an overall reorganization of the state-controlled sector of the economy seems to have been carried out early in 1952. This was designed to bring about a more rigid control of production and distribution. Under a directive of the Committee of Financial and Economic Affairs of January 1952 all state enterprises were to submit detailed inventories of their assets and quarterly plans for accelerating the turnover of their working capital. Under the 'Tentative Regulations Governing Capital Construction', the Committee was to issue sets of control figures together with appropriate instructions to the economic ministries and to regional economic organs. These would in turn send control figures and instructions to the units operating under their control. The operating units would draft annual plans which were to be examined and co-ordinated, first by the central economic ministries and regional economic organs, and then by the Committee on Financial and Economic Affairs. The co-ordinated plan which resulted from this process was to become, on approval by the State Administrative Council, the 'national capital construction plan'. It was then to be transmitted to the central economic ministries and regional economic organs and by them to the operating units responsible for the practical work of construction or manufacture.

In the autumn of 1952 it was announced that the first Five-Year Plan was to begin the next year. The State Planning Committee was established under Kao Kang, then chairman of the North-East Administrative Area. Planning organs were set up in all the economic ministries and in all government agencies, central and regional, having economic functions to discharge, including individual enterprises. There were created, in addition to the existing economic ministries (Agriculture, Commerce, Communications, Finance, Forestry, Fuel Industry, Heavy Industry, Light Industry, Railways, Telecommunications, Textile Industry, and Water Conservancy), six new ones (two Ministries of Machine Building, and the Ministries of Building Construction, Geology, Food, and Foreign Trade).

This machinery underwent various transformations during the course of the Plan. In 1954, when the new constitution was adopted, the State Planning Committee became the State Planning Commission and was placed under the newly constituted State Council or cabinet (possibly to prevent the new chairman, Li Fu-chun, from attaining too much power: Kao Kang had meanwhile been expelled from the Party for 'anti-Party activities' and was subsequently said to have committed suicide). The Commission was to be assisted by the State Statistical Bureau created in October 1952, whose head, Hsueh Mu-chiao, became concurrently vice-chairman of the State Planning Commission. At the same time the National Construction Commission was set up under Po I-po to supervise the capital-construction work of the Plan. The Ministry of Supervision was to inspect the carrying out of the Plan, check the accuracy of production reports, test the quality of products, examine accounts, and perform other similar tasks.

In May 1956 further changes were made. The short-term planning functions of the State Planning Commission, i.e. the formulation and supervision of the yearly plans and the day-to-day adjustments of planning targets that might be necessary, were taken over by a new body, the National Economic Commission, so that the State Planning Commission might be free to concentrate on long-term economic development. A General Supply Bureau was set up to co-ordinate the supply and distribution of building materials and raw products, over which difficulties were being experienced at that time. Finally a Technological Commission, on the lines of the Committee for New Technology in the Soviet Union, was created to supervise the adoption and popularization of new techniques and draw up plans for the future development of technology. In February 1958, the National Construction Commission was abolished and its work distributed between the State Planning Commission, the National Economic Commission, and the Ministry of Building.

The broad outline of economic planning in China follows the pattern established in the Soviet Union. But since the problems facing the régime in China differ from those with which the Soviet régime had to contend at a comparable period of

development, Soviet methods had to be modified in some ways
to meet the situation in China. One important difference
between the Soviet Union and the countries of Eastern Europe
on the one hand, and China on the other, was that in the
former the process of nationalization, except in the case of
agriculture and handicrafts, had been largely accomplished
before the launching of their first Five-Year Plans, though in
Eastern Europe domestic trade, particularly at the retail level,
also remained partly in private hands. In China, except for
parts of heavy industry and distribution, the economy was still
mainly in private hands when the first Five-Year Plan was
introduced in 1953. In 1952 the private sector of the economy,
according to official estimates, controlled over a third of the
total output of modern industries, nearly two-thirds of the total
trade turnover, and practically the entire output of agriculture.

The planning techniques adopted had to take account of this
fact, making use of methods most likely to produce the required
response from countless small, privately owned enterprises run
by independently minded Chinese business men. Thus the Plan
was to work in the private sector primarily through indirect
measures such as the control of raw materials, government
orders, tax policy, and price manipulation. By these means
private industry was gradually brought under the effective
control of the central planning machine and the way was
prepared for an eventual change in its ownership.

The contents of the first Five-Year Plan were not published
at the time of its announcement. The Plan itself probably did
not at first contain any fully worked-out and detailed programme of development in individual industries such as are laid
down in the Soviet Five-Year Plans.[1] No specific production
targets under the Plan, other than the annual production goals
which had existed in previous years, were announced until two
and a half years after it had been launched.

The main principles governing the Plan were set out in a
People's Daily editorial of 16 September 1953. They were:

1. The development of the capital-goods industries should be
such as to promote the rapid growth of heavy industry.

[1] Cf. Li Fu-chun's report on the Five-Year Plan to the National People's
Congress on 5 and 6 July 1955 (BBC, Econ. Suppl., 14 July 1955).

2. The rate of growth of the capital-goods industries should exceed that of the consumer-goods industries.

3. The development of agriculture should be directed to ensuring adequate supplies of grain and industrial raw materials, and to increasing the agricultural surplus with which to finance industrialization.

4. The rate of growth in labour productivity should be greater than the rise in wages in order to ensure accumulation of capital.

5. New industrial centres should be established close to raw-material supplies.

Stress was also laid on the need to make the maximum use of the Soviet Union's 'advanced experience' in implementing the Plan.

In his report on the work of the Government to the First National People's Congress of 23 September 1954 Chou En-lai admitted that, even then, the blueprint of the first Five-Year Plan was 'not yet complete and final', and many of its details were being supplemented and amended. And in a report to the National People's Congress of 5 and 6 July 1955 Li Fu-chun, Deputy Premier and chairman of the State Planning Commission, said that the work of drawing up the draft Plan, which had begun in 1951, was not completed, after repeated revision, until February 1955, two years after the Plan had been put into operation.

The fact is that the Chinese authorities were clearly not in a position to institute a Five-Year Plan in 1953. They had neither the administrative capacity, the planning technique, nor the statistical knowledge and machinery. They were driven by ambition and ideology to name 1953 as the opening year of a Five-Year Plan. But in fact a Plan in the proper sense of the word could not begin until these deficiencies had been made good. During the early years the Government carried on the system of production targets for individual industries, expressed in terms of a percentage increase over the previous year, which had already existed before. No doubt individual enterprises were kept more closely under the control of the central Government and their activities more carefully co-ordinated with other

sectors of the same industry and of related industries than
before. But a Plan, in the sense that the word is used in the
Soviet Union, a detailed blueprint showing the projected
development, stage by stage, of each individual section of the
economy over a considerable period to come, does not seem to
have existed at this time. There was thus never a First Five-
Year Plan in the proper sense of the word; there was, rather,
a Two-and-a-half-Year Plan formulated during the first half of
1955 and announced in July of that year, drawn up partly in
the light of the results already achieved during the first two
years of the period nominally covered by the Plan.

Early in 1955 the drafting of the Plan was sponsored by the
Central Committee of the CCP and it was discussed, and
generally approved, by a National Conference of the Party in
March 1955. The draft Plan was passed, after some revision, to
the State Council on 10 June 1955. It was adopted by the State
Council on 18 June 1955, and was then submitted to the second
session of the National People's Congress for examination and
approval.

A report on the Plan was made to the Congress on 5 and
6 July 1955 by Li Fu-chun, a Deputy Premier and chairman
of the State Planning Commission. The 'fundamental task' of
the Plan was described as the concentration of the country's
main efforts in industrial construction on 694 particularly vital
enterprises, of which the most important were 156 plants to be
designed and built by the Soviet Union. Other fundamental
tasks were the introduction of co-operative farms in agriculture,
and the incorporation of private industry and commerce into
various forms of state capitalist organization, thus 'laying the
groundwork for the socialist transformation of private industry
and commerce'.

The main target of the Plan was given in Li Fu-chun's report
as roughly to double industrial output. Outlay on economic
construction and 'cultural and educational development' was
to be 76,640 million yuan.[1] Of this total, 55·8 per cent., or
42,740 million yuan, was intended for investment in capital
construction, including development for agriculture, forestry,

---

[1] These figures are expressed in terms of the new yuan established by the
currency conversions of March 1955. See below, p. 44, n. 2.

Distribution of Investment in First Five-Year Plan

	'000 million yuan	Per cent. of total
Industrial ministries	24·85	58·2
Agriculture, forestry, & water conservancy	3·26	7·6
Transport, posts, & telecommunications	8·21	19·2
Trade, banking, & stockpiling	1·28	3·0
Culture, education, & public health	3·08	7·2
Development of municipal public utilities	1·60	3·7
Others	0·46	1·1

Source: First Five-Year Plan, p. 29.

education, public health, trading and financial enterprises, public utilities, &c.; while the rest was to be spent on prospecting for resources, surveying and designing schemes, supply work preparatory to basic construction, transport and communications, large-scale repair of equipment, measures for improving techniques and organization, experimental production of new items, buying of fixed property, 'circulating capital' for the economic departments, and expenditure by the economic, cultural, and educational departments on the training of specialized cadres for managerial posts.

Firm priority was given to the capital industries. During the course of the plan, investment in 'means of production' was to account for 88·8 per cent. of total investment in industry.[1] Output value of capital production was planned to increase by 126·5 per cent. while that of production for the consumer sector was to grow by only 79·7 per cent. The share of the consumer sector in output would drop from 60·3 per cent. in 1952 to 54·6 per cent. in 1957, while the share of the output of capital goods in the aggregate value of industrial output would rise from 39·7 per cent. in 1952 to 45·5 per cent. in 1957. The Plan provided for a rapid increase in the proportion of total production achieved by the state-owned industries. Output of the private sector was planned to fall from 41 per cent. of the total value of industrial output in 1952 to 12·2 per cent. in 1957, while the output value of the state, co-operative, and joint state-private sectors was to rise to 87·8 per cent.

[1] This proportion was later revised. See below, p. 53.

These plans were highly ambitious. The production of steel was to be more than trebled, and that of coal and electricity about doubled, within five years. Other targets were not much less bold. Comparisons with the Indian first Five-Year Plan are misleading, because China probably started from a more backward position; but for what it is worth, the Chinese aim of

Production Targets under the Plan

(million tons)

	Pre-Communist production peak (incl. Manchuria)	1952 output	1957 (Plan)	Percentage increase 1957 over 1952
Coal	61·9	63·5	113·0	178
Pig-iron	1·8	1·9	4·6	246
Steel	0·9	1·35	4·12	306
Electricity (billion kwh.)	6·0	7·26	15·9	219
Crude oil	0·3	0·43	2·01	462
Cement	2·3	2·86	6·0	210
Cotton cloth (m. bolts)	41·0	111·65	164·0	147

Sources: Proposals for Second Five-Year Plan; Handbook on People's China (Peking, 1957).

increasing national income by about 43 per cent. may be compared with the Indian aim of an increase of 11 per cent.

China perhaps had a slight temporary advantage over India in the amount of foreign aid she could count on.[1] Soviet assistance was of course crucial for the success of the Plan. In her lack of capital equipment, investment funds, and technicians, China was in some ways in a similar position to the Soviet Union herself on the eve of her first Five-Year Plan in 1928.[2] But the Soviet Union had then already an industrial basis on which to build, and was better equipped with technical staff and skilled workers than China. China, on the other hand, was able to some extent to make good these deficiencies through

[1] See below, p. 77.
[2] For a detailed comparison of the economic position of China in 1953 with that of the Soviet Union in 1928 see W. W. Rostow, *The Prospects for Communist China* (New York, Praeger, 1956), pp. 258–62.

Russian help, instead of being obliged, like the Soviet Union, to rely on the few Western technicians who were prepared to make themselves available.

The 156 new enterprises which were to be built with the aid of the Soviet Union[1] were thus of vital importance, not only in themselves, but because they were to provide the Chinese with the necessary technical foundation for developing a modern industrial economy. The Plan envisaged that 60 per cent. of the basic construction work would be designed by Soviet experts, and the remainder by Chinese planners working under the guidance of Soviet specialists. What the Chinese designers particularly needed was experience in 'whole-set designing', i.e. designing for large-scale and integrated manufacturing processes; hitherto Chinese experience had been mainly concerned with relatively simple workshops or parts of factories and mines. The training of large numbers of scientific and technical personnel was described in Li Fu-chun's report as one of the 'major tasks' of the first and second Five-Year Plans. And it may well be that China's long-term industrial future will depend more on her capacity to master the advanced techniques required by modern industrial methods than on her success in achieving any of the other ambitious targets she has set herself in her first Five-Year Plans.

Russian help in the provision of capital resources was an even more important asset to the Chinese. These were supplied not mainly in liquid form but in the form of the individual enterprises which the Russians built. The total value of the 156 enterprises was about 3,000 million yuan at the official rate of exchange, equivalent to about 6 per cent. of Chinese investment in capital construction during the course of the Plan. The need for capital investment could only partly be met by aid from the Soviet Union, however. For the most part the Government were dependent for capital resources on internal saving, in the form of taxation, the profits of government enterprises, subscriptions to bond issues, and other types of forced loan.

The budgets announced in the early years of the Plan showed that the Chinese Government were taking steps to bring about a supply of capital from such sources. The revenue projected

[1] See below, pp. 72–73.

from the profits of state enterprises was half as high again in 1953 as in the previous year, and by 1955 was more than double the 1952 figure. By this time such profits accounted for more than two-thirds of total revenue. Non-agricultural taxation (i.e. principally taxation on industrial enterprises) also rose sharply in the 1953 budget, and by 1954 was nearly double the 1952 figure. By the end of the first Five-Year Plan levies on industry in the form of taxation and profits (the revenue from these is roughly equal) together accounted for about 80 per cent. of total government revenues.

Agricultural taxation remained fairly steady, though under the system of compulsory deliveries at fixed prices the peasants may have been contributing more as a result of reduced profit margins, thus enabling the state trading enterprises to increase their profits. Agricultural taxation represented about 7 per cent. of the budget in 1957. It is claimed that the taxation paid by the peasants has declined as a proportion of their income, though this claim has little significance in itself; the significant figure is the proportion represented by taxation and deliveries together.

Under new regulations issued in February 1958 agricultural taxation is to remain steady at the absolute level of 1958 throughout the second Five-Year Plan, so that the proportion of tax to each farm's output should drop from about $11 \cdot 31$ in 1957 to $7 \cdot 1$ by 1962 at the rate of growth in agricultural production then envisaged. If this level is in fact maintained, and the figures for the recent harvests are anywhere near reliable, the proportion should in fact go down to very much less than this.

Taxation on the joint state-private enterprises accounted for another 7 per cent. of revenue in 1957. The other 6 per cent. came from loan income and other sources. The total revenue increased from 189,278 billion[1] yuan (old rate of exchange)[2] in 1952 to 292,139 billion (about £4,500 million) in 1957.[3] Current budgets, though covering a wider proportion of the economy, are roughly equivalent in volume, in monetary terms, to British budgets.

[1] Billion=1,000 million throughout.
[2] The official rate of exchange was 68,599 yuan=£1 in Dec. 1952. In 1955 the Chinese Government knocked four noughts off their currency, and the present rate is 6·859 yuan=£1.
[3] See table on facing page.

Summary of Draft Budget, 1957

('000 yuan)

Revenue		Expenditure	
Taxation	14,570,209	Economic construction*	13,683,051
State enterprises	13,668,969	Social services, culture & education	4,835,216
Loans	623,320	Defence	5,523,320
Other sources	430,436	Administration	2,445,314
		Loan payments	829,044
		Aid to foreign countries	507,980
		Other expenditure	275,344
		Transfer to credit fund	600,000
		General reserve	593,755
Total	29,292,934	Total	29,292,934

* Subdivided as follows: industry 8,121,256; agriculture 2,044,396; communications 2,216,442; trade 256,922.

Source: Minister of Finance, Budget Report to National People's Congress, 29 June 1957 (*NCNA*, Suppl. No. 254, 3 July 1957).

In general the Communists have made great efforts to balance their budgets, probably because of their realization of the large contribution that unbalanced budgets before the war made to the inflation of that period. This did not, however, prevent a fairly substantial deficit being incurred in 1956, a year of excessive economic expansion. There has usually been a substantial carry-over of unexpended revenue from one year to the next. Total expenditure increased at the same rate as revenue, less these surpluses, amounting to about 30,000 or 40,000 billion yuan a year (old rate of exchange). Total expenditure planned for 'national construction' roughly doubled for the first three years of the Plan from about 73,000 billion yuan in 1952 to 142,000 billion in 1955. Planned expenditure on social, cultural, and educational activities and on defence showed smaller increases, while the amount set aside for administration and other purposes remained, in absolute terms, roughly stable.

Budgets in Communist countries normally cover a large proportion of the total national income, though in the less industrialized countries this proportion is not so big. During

the first Five-Year Plan the proportion in China was around
30 per cent., roughly the same as in the United Kingdom.[1]

Approximately half the budget is devoted to 'economic construction'. About four-fifths of this goes to capital investment.
Expenditure on defence rose sharply during the Korean War,
subsequently declined to around 20 per cent. of the total budget
in 1954–7, and is now declining slightly both relatively and
absolutely. The proportion of expenditure on defence and
administration to total expenditure is intended to decline from
about 32 per cent. in the period 1952–7 to 20 per cent. in
1958–62.

At the Congress of the CCP in November 1956 Po I-po gave
the following figures (in percentages) for the proportion of
'capital accumulation' in the national income during the period
1952–6:

1952	1953	1954	1955	1956
15·7	18·3	21·6	20·5	22·8

He said that for some years to come, given normal conditions,
the proportion of capital accumulation in the total national
income would probably be somewhat more than 20 per cent.
The proportion of the state budget in the national income,
which between 1952 and 1956 had varied between 27·6 and
32·4 per cent., should normally amount to no less than, and
possibly more than, 30 per cent. Of the income from the state
budget, at least 70 per cent. would probably continue to come
from the state-run industries.

The important figure therefore is the proportion of the state
budget which the Government devote to capital construction.
During the years 1952 to 1956, this proportion was as follows
(in percentages):

1952	1953	1954	1955	–1956
29·9	37·9	38·9	35·6	46·7

Capital construction in 1956 had been 62 per cent. larger
than in the previous year. It is fairly clear that Po I-po regarded
the proportion of the budget devoted to capital investment in

[1] In 1957 the values of both national income and budget revenue were, on the
basis of the official exchange rate, about equal in the two countries: roughly
£17,000 million and £5,000 million respectively. But the figures do not, of course,
furnish any useful comparison of economic realities in the two countries.

1956 as excessive. The whole balance of the economy had been affected as a result. On the whole, Po I-po thought, capital construction should account for about 40 per cent., or a little over, of the state budget. This would allow a margin to enable the level of consumption to rise slowly, and should at the same time ensure an adequate rate of industrial expansion.

In the event a shortage of revenue was not to prove the major difficulty of the Chinese Government in carrying out the first Five-Year Plan. Indeed, the principal crisis which they faced during its execution arose rather from an excessive rate of investment and the consequent threat to the stability of the economy.

V

THE FIRST FIVE-YEAR PLAN

DESPITE the exuberant tone of the speeches made at the time of its inauguration, the first Five-Year Plan in fact made an inauspicious start. Already in January 1953 it was announced that the original targets for construction work set for that year under the Plan were to be reduced by 30 per cent. (although no indication was then given of what the targets were). In May there was a reduction of some of the production targets, first announced by Chou En-lai in February. In the first eight months of 1953 only half the annual target for capital construction contained in the investment programme was fulfilled, and many individual industries and enterprises failed to achieve their targets for industrial production in the first half of the year. There were sharp criticisms of these failures, and especially of inadequate planning and administrative confusion, in the press. In September further reductions of the targets appear to have been made.

A combination of factors seems to have been responsible for these failures. Among the most important internal causes were weather calamities, which throughout 1953 had a serious effect on agricultural production, varying in intensity in different parts of China. Other difficulties were created by competing demands for labour, particularly for technicians and managers, and for materials essential for construction. But the principal trouble was undoubtedly inefficient and over-ambitious planning by individual enterprises. In April 1953 the *People's Daily* demanded: 'Do not bite off more than you can chew', and in July there were many references in the press to 'adventurist progress' in new construction. This over-enthusiastic construction work resulted in the wastage of investment funds and bottlenecks in the supply of materials. Many factories and mines were blamed for 'chaotic industrial management' in failing to fulfil their targets for the first six months of the year. Even factories which had fulfilled their targets had often done so, it was alleged, by 'shock operations' which resulted in many accidents, fluctuations in quality, and inadequately maintained equipment.

The main external factor affecting fulfilment of the Plan was the delay in reaching final agreement on the scale of Soviet aid. The commercial agreement for the current year (including the annual protocol to the 300 million dollar loan agreement reached in May 1950) was not arranged until March 1953. And it took until September 1953 to settle the arrangements for Soviet aid for the Plan itself.[1]

The result of this combination of factors was that there were many miscalculations, and production targets for some branches of industry could not be met. Although it was later claimed that the Plan for 1953 was over-fulfilled and that the value of industrial output was 13 per cent. higher than in 1952, it is clear that serious difficulties were encountered during the year, and that the authorities were by no means satisfied with the way the Plan was progressing. There were complaints that many production plans were still inaccurate, ill co-ordinated, or revised too frequently, and that there was not enough co-operation between related departments and enterprises. In addition there was not enough control of capital and overhead costs.

Thus at the beginning of 1954 Chinese industry was called on to remedy the defects made evident during the first year's working of the Plan. One of the principal failings which the authorities were trying to combat was the tendency of individual industries and enterprises to concentrate their energies and resources on new development, the construction of new plants and other units of production, while tending to neglect the importance of already existing enterprises. This was one aspect of the general tendency towards over-expansion, which accentuated the inflationary effects inevitably associated with a rapidly developing economy. These inflationary trends were the more serious in China, where the first efforts towards industrialization coincided with the pressures engendered by the Korean War.

One of the measures adopted by the Government to assist in the accomplishment of production goals at this time was a

[1] See below, p. 79.

campaign to encourage the introduction of technical innovations. All industries were exhorted to learn from the Soviet
Union's 'advanced experience' in the industrial field. The
Government were anxious to persuade Chinese managers and
technical staffs to derive every possible benefit from the advice
of the Soviet technical advisers, and to study in the trade and
technical journals the most up-to-date methods. This injunction
applied to every conceivable operation in all fields of work,
from the installation of seamless-steel tubing mills to the operation of tug-drawn barges on the Yangtze, in all of which Soviet
methods were said to be incomparably superior to any other.

The year 1954 was in many ways the calmest of any single
year under the present régime. The Korean War was over,
there was no immediate prospect of any other hostilities in
which China might be engaged elsewhere, and the new Government participated for the first time at an international conference (the Geneva Conference) as an equal partner with
other major world powers: there was therefore no longer any
need to devote such a large part of the nation's scanty economic
resources to defence purposes. For almost the first time since
the régime started, there was no violent internal political campaign to unsettle and distract the population. Conditions were
therefore economically fairly favourable, though the country
was still suffering from the effects of the floods which had
occurred the year before, and there were further, even more
serious floods in 1954. Thus economic development seems to
have gone ahead more smoothly than the previous year. At the
end of the year an increase in industrial production of 17 per
cent. over 1953 was claimed.

The Five-Year Plan itself seems to have remained in a somewhat tentative stage. Its first two years were essentially ones of
exploration in the technique of large-scale economic planning,
and of practice in the making of accurate and balanced estimates of the country's resources. One thing that became clear
was that a pre-condition of such work was the development of
an adequate statistical service to measure the available
resources. The provision of better and more detailed statistics
was set as one of the main targets of 1955.

During the next year the attention of the Government seems

to have been mainly concentrated on agriculture; in the summer of 1955 the sudden violent spurt in collectivization was initiated. At the end of the year there occurred a similar movement for the incorporation of private business in state-private organizations covering the whole of an industry in a given locality. Although the fact that the Government felt free to develop these critical and politically dangerous campaigns in close succession was itself an indication that they were not experiencing any very serious difficulties at home, the campaigns cannot have been without their unsettling effect.

The Government were also handicapped by the effects of the natural calamities of the two previous years. These affected economic development not only by obliging the Government to transfer labour and resources to the work of rehabilitation, but also because, on the one hand, by reducing the available exports of agricultural produce they probably cut down imports of equipment from the Soviet Union, and on the other, as a result of the lower profits on agricultural produce and the consumer-goods industries, they reduced the funds available for capital investment at home. In fact, figures given by Po I-po in a speech to the Eighth Congress of the CCP in November 1956 revealed that the volume of capital construction in 1955, expressed as a proportion of the state budget, dropped considerably from the rate of the previous two years.[1]

It is clear that the Government were having some difficulty in getting the investment programme fully under way at this time. The total level of capital construction by the end of 1955 was still running well below the level that would have been necessary to achieve an evenly spaced programme over the whole Plan. According to the *People's Daily* of 18 March 1956, only just over 50 per cent. of the capital-construction programme had been accomplished up till then. This meant that capital investment to the value of nearly 22,000 million yuan would have to be undertaken in 1956 and 1957, or an annual rate for the remainder of the Plan of 11,000 million yuan. During 1955 the value of capital investment had been about 8,000 million yuan. Thus a considerable spurt in the volume of investment was needed to fulfil the target for the Plan as a whole.

[1] See above, p. 46.

As it turned out, during the next year the target was easily exceeded, and with very nearly disastrous results. The 1956 budget revealed the headlong rate of expansion that the Government were aiming at in that year: 14,000 million yuan were to be spent on capital construction, an increase of about 62 per cent. over the previous year. This was about one-third of the total provided for in the Five-Year Plan. An increase in the total value of industrial and agricultural production of 14·1 per cent. was planned, as against 6·6 per cent. the year before—a very high target indeed. By June it was being said that the level of industrial production planned for the end of the Five-Year Plan in 1957 would probably be reached by the end of 1956. Output of twenty-eight out of the forty-six major industrial products was said to have already either reached or exceeded 1957 levels. Agricultural production would probably also reach the Five-Year Plan figure in 1956.

But the Plan was clearly running into serious difficulties at this time. With the rapid increase in the pace of development, shortages of some materials, especially cement and steel products for construction, began to make themselves felt. This seems to have been quite simply a result of faulty planning. The planned increases in production of these products were inadequate to make possible the amounts of construction work which were being provided for at the time. Thus delays occurred which caused further difficulties in other sectors.

It seems likely too that to some extent the spectacular increases in production which were being made were achieved at the expense of the quality of the products turned out. One of the recurring themes of the Chinese press and government spokesmen during this period was the need to ensure that high standards of quality were not sacrificed for the sake of bigger output and of exceeding production targets. It is clear that there was still a great deal of over-ambitious expansion by individual enterprises. Some seem to have made sure of exceeding their targets only by the lavish and uneconomical expenditure of capital, and unnecessarily large overhead costs. There were increasingly urgent calls for the most economical possible use of the limited supply of available capital.

As a result of these strains various adjustments took place.

The Government decided, probably as a result of the big wages increase given in the spring of that year[1] and of the inflationary pressure which the current frantic rate of expansion was generating, to make some adjustment in the ratio between investment in light and in heavy industry. It was decided that, in the last two years of the Plan, the proportion should be altered to a ratio between heavy and light of 7:1 as against 8:1 originally planned. The profits of the light industries providing consumer goods could be used for investment, and a larger supply of consumer goods would reduce the inflationary effects of the heavy volume of investment still being maintained.

Other relaxations were introduced. On 5 July 1956 Chen Yun recommended to the National People's Congress the adoption of a new system of trading within the state trading mechanism corresponding in the field of industry to the system of free markets being introduced in the agricultural field. Instead of automatically purchasing all the products of a factory, for certain commodities the commercial departments would retain freedom of choice to buy or reject the produce of a factory according to the state of consumer demand. In some cases the factories could sell what remained to the commercial departments on a commission basis, or they could themselves dispose of their products in competition with the state trading departments. At the same time the wholesale departments could not expect to be able to distribute the goods they had bought to the retail agencies irrespective of the choice of those agencies, who must be free to accept or reject the goods they were offered in accordance with consumer demand in the area they served. Many of the controls imposed on the former capitalist enterprises, now virtually taken over by the state, were to be relaxed. More flexible banking arrangements should be made available, and there should be more genuinely free competition.

Thus it appears that the authorities had been made aware of the rigidity and unresponsiveness to consumer demand of the old system, and were genuinely anxious to do what they could to give a better deal to the consumer, if only to increase the profits of the trading agencies. The move would also probably

[1] See below, p. 120.

have the effect of increasing the effectiveness of incentive payments and so of raising productivity.

Nevertheless, towards the end of 1956, the signs of strain in the economy were becoming increasingly evident. There were ever more strident complaints about shortages of materials and about hoarding by enterprises which had become uncertain of their supplies. In addition to the continuing deficiencies of steel and building materials, there was beginning to be a critical shortage of coal. Although coal output in 1956 was said to be about 60 per cent. higher than in 1953, demand, for both industrial and domestic consumption, had increased even more. A directive called on all government offices, troops, and schools to reduce the coal used for heating and cooking by 15 to 25 per cent. Coal miners, some of whom were already working on Sundays, were asked voluntarily to give up two days of their Chinese New Year holiday of three days (representing nearly half their total holiday for the year) in order to maintain production—a suggestion which the miners were reported to have greeted 'with the most joyful enthusiasm'.

There was much criticism of the over-expansion that had taken place in the industrial field. It was recognized that the development of industry over the last few years had been excessive in relation to that of agriculture. Li Fu-chun, the chairman of the State Planning Commission, admitted that its work had been 'grossly inadequate'.[1] Too much attention had been paid to large-scale state industry and not enough to local industry, agriculture, and commerce. Thus, for example, the level of agricultural development had been allowed to lag behind the needs of consumption. In the effort to develop new industrial areas in the interior, the development of the coastal areas, e.g. Shanghai, had been neglected. There had also been an imbalance in the relationship between labour productivity and wages.

It is fairly clear that, although 1956 was without doubt in the industrial field the most successful year for the régime of any since it came into power—industrial output was said to have increased by 25 per cent. over 1955, capital investment by 60 per cent., and the production of many industries to have

[1] *NCNA*, 27 May 1957.

reached or neared the 1957 targets—these successes were achieved only at the expense of severely over-extending the economy. The inordinately high rate of capital construction, which reached 14,000 million yuan (£2,000 million at the official rate of exchange), 60 per cent. higher than the previous year, taken in conjunction with the fairly substantial wage increases granted during the year, brought about strong inflationary pressures. During the following year it was revealed that there had been a budget deficit of 1,830 million yuan (about £260 million) in 1956. This was attributed by Li Hsiennien, Minister of Finance, to flood-relief expenditure, overfulfilment of capital projects, and the wage increases in the early part of this year. In addition the budget surpluses of previous years, which had been reckoned as revenue in the preparation of the budget, had been transferred to the Bank of China, which on the strength of these had increased its rate of lending to the peasants and the handicraft and state-private enterprises, so that these loans reached a figure more than double that planned. The number of workers increased during the year by 2·3 million instead of 800,000 as intended, while 600,000 were being supported at technical schools and universities; consequently the wage bill rose by 2,400 million yuan in a year. As a result of these developments the state was obliged to increase the note issue by about 1,700 million yuan more than the increase in commodities in circulation. To relieve the inflationary pressure the commercial departments had been obliged to release 2,000 million yuan worth of stockpiled materials held in reserve.[1]

Thus the Chinese authorities had not escaped the problems which have caused difficulties for all the other Communist countries, and indeed nearly all underdeveloped countries— that of how to secure a very rapid rate of development for heavy industry while at the same time providing a sufficient supply of consumer goods to relieve the inflationary pressures inevitably generated by this process. At the beginning of 1957 the Government, having already virtually achieved the goals of the Five-Year Plan, began to slow down the pace. It was

[1] The total value of these stockpiled materials was revealed as 20,000–30,000 million yuan.

officially accepted that production in 1957 would be little above
that of 1956. Investment programmes were to be cut. There
was to be a big increase in consumer production during the
next year, to mop up some of the surplus spending power
brought about by the new wage rates. For the same reason the
workers and peasants were to take up a larger proportion of the
Government's savings bonds. Industrial enterprises were called
upon to lay off some of the excessive labour force they had
recruited during the past year. Drastic reductions in building
work were announced. Loans to peasants were to be reduced.
And there was to be a cut in military expenditure.

The 1957 budget reflected the sharp slowing down of the rate
of expansion. There was to be a decrease of 4 per cent. in
expenditure and an increase of 2 per cent. in revenue. Investment in capital construction was to be reduced to 11,100
million yuan, 20 per cent. less than in 1956 but 1,400 million
more than originally planned for 1957 in the Five-Year Plan.
The value of industrial output would increase by only 4·5 per
cent. over 1956 and that of agricultural production by 4·9
per cent.

One of the forms taken by the campaign for retrenchment
was a big cutting-down of administrative staffs both in government offices and in industrial enterprises. This movement was
closely linked with the 'rectification' policy ushered in by Mao
Tse-tung in February 1957. This was carried on vigorously in
the factories and farms throughout that year. Workers were
encouraged to voice their criticisms of the administrations of
the factories, and to make suggestions for improvements in
techniques. One of the principal demands made by the workers,
no doubt at the instigation of the Communist Party, was for a
reduction of unproductive staff. A large-scale exodus of cadres,
Communist Party workers, students, and intellectuals, to the
country, where they were to 'join the people', followed, and
140,000 cadres were said to have left from Shanghai alone.

Announcements at the end of 1957 claimed that the Five-
Year Plan had been over-fulfilled by 17 per cent., and the Plan
for capital construction by 13 per cent. These are figures for
increases in the value of production 'at fixed prices of 1952';
and, as analysis of Soviet figures has shown, any assessment in

these terms lends itself to big distortions according to the system of pricing employed.[1] Production of steel was reported to have reached 5,240,000 tons, of iron 5,860,000 tons, of electric power 19,030 million kwh. (each about 25 per cent. above the target), of coal 122,440,000 tons (about 8 per cent. above), and of oil 1,420,000 tons (only about two-thirds of the original target). Grain production was said to have increased by 30 million tons and cotton by 335,000 tons since the beginning of the Plan. The food-grain production plan had been over-fulfilled by 11·6 per cent. Total investment for the five years had exceeded that originally planned by about 5,000 million yuan.

A number of new achievements in the industrial field were announced. Production of 'liberation' lorries started at the No. 1 motor works Changchun in the autumn of 1956. Production of a light civil aircraft, the AN-2, to be used primarily for crop-spraying, surveying, and photographing, is said to have begun in December 1957. A Chinese-built oil-tanker of 4,500 tons was launched in the same year. It was also announced during 1957 that China could now design without outside assistance large-scale iron and steel complexes with an output of 1½ million tons a year, hydro-electric stations of up to 1 million tons, shipyards for the construction of ocean-going vessels, steam-turbine and boiler factories, and diesel-engine works. Trial production of a 40,000 kva.transformer, a 72,500 kw. hydro-electric generator, 25,000 kw. thermal-generating equipment, heat-resisting alloy steel, and other products was claimed.

Achievement in the Plan was clearly uneven. First, the increase in agricultural production, though said to have exceeded the target, was not only certainly below what it should have been to keep pace with the increase in industrial production; it was probably barely enough to maintain the living standards of the rapidly increasing Chinese population, let alone to provide a surplus for export on the scale required. Secondly, within the field of industrial production, while certain items, such as iron, steel, and electricity production, had been developed even more rapidly than the original

[1] From 1958 onwards Chinese figures of production value are to be in terms of 'fixed 1957 prices'.

ambitious programme had planned, for others, such as oil, it
had been found very difficult even to approach the levels of
production that had been hoped for.

In addition, the Chinese leaders had found that a very rapid
rate of development, such as that achieved in 1956, produced
inflationary pressures that they were not in a position to meet,
except by reducing the rate of development and increasing the
proportion of resources devoted to consumer-goods production.
They had become conscious that too great an emphasis had
been given to the development of large-scale enterprises, requir-
ing big amounts of capital but economical in labour, which is
plentiful, while not enough attention had been given to the
building of smaller and less modern plants.[1] These were the
principal lessons which the Chinese planners had to take into
account when they began to formulate their plans for the
further development of the Chinese economy.

[1] See below, p. 64.

VI

THE GREAT LEAP FORWARD

THE resolution on the political report[1] which was passed at the end of the Congress of the CCP in September 1956 set out some of the aims which were to guide the Party in their direction of the economy over the next few years. The resolution reaffirmed the policy of giving priority to the development of heavy industry. It called for the vigorous expansion of the metallurgical, engineering, power, coal, oil, chemical, and building-materials industries, and stressed in particular the importance of those branches of heavy industry which were still lacking or undeveloped, but which were urgently needed: thus it demanded improvements in the manufacture of high-grade alloy steels, and in the refining of rare metals, and called for the setting up of an organic synthetic-chemical industry, a radio-engineering industry, and an atomic-energy industry.

In agriculture, since there was little prospect of developing an agricultural-machinery industry or a chemical-fertilizer industry on any scale within the near future, efforts would be concentrated on various methods of improving yields, such as improving farming methods, use of better seeds, irrigation work, popularization of the use of new implements, improvement of the soil, and prevention of plant diseases and pests. Transport and commerce should be developed in step with the development of industry and agriculture. The resolution emphasized the importance of maintaining standards of quality as well as of quantity, a point that has clearly been exercising the Chinese in recent years. This is no doubt a result of the shoddy quality of much material turned out in the effort to over-fulfil production norms.

One of the most important features of the resolution was the recommendation that a certain level of production of some commodities would be carried on outside the provisions of the Plan, and would be produced 'directly' by the production units

[1] *NCNA*, Suppl. No. 248, 1 Oct. 1956.

in accordance with the supply of materials and the market situation. Similarly, it was recognized that there were some factories and shops which would not necessarily benefit from centralized control, and should retain a fair degree of economic autonomy. Such units should be placed under the control of 'dispersed management' rather than centralized management. This consideration was to be especially borne in mind in the reorganization of the joint state-private and small-scale private businesses. Even pedlars and other small traders should be allowed to carry on their businesses in the residential areas of towns and villages. These decisions, coupled with the decision to restore a limited free market in the field of agricultural marketing and the increased freedom of choice within the state trading mechanism, are an indication that the authorities were already beginning to adjust their policies to economic requirements, even where such action appeared to conflict with their own preconceived theories. They are interesting, too, in that they reflect a similar trend to that shown in the measures of economic decentralization recently introduced in the Soviet Union.

The recommendation for greater decentralization and for more autonomy for individual enterprises was implemented in the new regulations on industrial control published in November 1957. These removed the control of many industries from the industrial ministries in Peking to those of provincial and local administrations. Some enterprises previously controlled by the Ministries of Light Industry and of Food were placed under the control of the provinces, autonomous regions, and municipalities under the direct control of the central Government (that is the second-tier authorities). All construction enterprises, some transport undertakings, and all factories other than heavy industry enterprises, such as large mines, power installations, iron and steel works, heavy and precision machinery factories, oil refineries, &c., were to be transferred to the lower (third-tier) authorities: but the second-tier authorities would retain some centralized control over the construction enterprises. Even those enterprises remaining under the management of the central departments would be under the 'dual leadership' of the central and regional (second-tier) authorities.

Further powers were also delegated to the local authorities

for the allocation of materials. The materials needed by enterprises under the ministries or by the second-tier authorities, or
by the commercial agencies, would still be controlled either by
the National Economic Commission or by individual ministries.
But the materials needed by local government (third-tier)
operated enterprises were to be allocated by the second-tier
authorities.

The total profits of the transferred enterprises would be
distributed in the ratio of 20 per cent. to the local authority
concerned, and 80 per cent. to the central Government.
Regional authorities were to have greater power in controlling
the direction of investment, provided that they kept within the
prescribed limitations of volume. They were also to have wider
powers over movements of personnel even within enterprises
still controlled by the ministries.

Local authorities were also given increased powers to
found and run their own commercial organizations. Wholesale
purchasing and distribution stations, warehouses and large
refrigeration plants established by the commercial departments
would fall under the 'dual leadership of the central and local
authorities'. All processing establishments affiliated to the
various commercial departments were to be transferred to the
local authorities and placed under the direct control of the local
commercial departments, though their production standards
would still be subject to control by the central Government.
The State Council would announce only four targets for commerce for the local authorities: purchasing plans, sales plans,
the total number of workers, and the amount of profits, and
would allow a 5 per cent. latitude in the implementing of the
sales and purchase plans. Local authorities would also have
powers over the sale and purchase of agricultural products,
grain, cotton, oils, &c. Individual enterprises were to have no
fixed goals for profits; the object of this was apparently that
they should not attempt to lower or raise purchasing or sales
prices to achieve a particular target. Commercial departments,
moreover, would have to pay the local authorities 20 per cent.
of their profits. Regional authorities, in addition, were to get
a cut for certain types of transactions relating to foreign trade.

At the same time as this transfer of control to the regional and local authorities, provision was made for a considerable increase in the powers of the managements of the individual enterprises. The number of targets set by the central ministries for production enterprises would be reduced to four: the volume of production, the number of workers, the total amount of wages, and the level of profits retained. Outside these fields managements would have power to fix and alter their plans as they wished, though their decisions must be reported. In a few cases, however, the central ministries were empowered to add other targets covering, for example, the trial production of new products. The procedure for formulating plans was to be simplified to reduce paper-work. Under the new system the higher-level authority would issue control figures (covering targets of volume, &c.), the lower level would then draw up a plan, and this would be finalized at the higher level.

Profits were to be shared between the state (and in some cases the local authority) on the one hand, and the individual enterprises on the other, according to a complicated formula, taking account of the investment needs of individual enterprises, a cash bonus for achievement, and the proportion (normally 40 per cent.) of their profits which they had been allowed to retain during the first Five-Year Plan. The exact ratio for each enterprise would be decided by the ministry concerned. Each enterprise would have the power to dispose of its profits as it wished, 'using the larger proportion on production' and some on welfare for the worker. It might increase, decrease, or scrap its property according to the functional power bestowed on it by the higher authorities. All enterprises were given power to hire and fire all their own employees except leading management and technical staff; but they were not permitted to increase the total number of workers.

During 1958 it was announced that 80 per cent. of the enterprises formerly handled by the industrial ministries had been handed over to the local authorities. These included all textile and virtually all light-industry factories, and a large proportion of those under the Ministry of Heavy Industry. It was said that the central Government would concentrate their efforts on the running of a small number of special enterprises, including those of a very large size, the provision of overall planning and co-ordination, and the study and popularization of techniques discovered by experimental methods. In June 1958 a new set of regulations was published, transferring the power to issue bonds entirely to the local authorities, who were to use them to raise capital for their industrial development. Local governments were also given control of the proceeds of certain taxes previously accruing to the central Government. Finally, in July 1958, further measures were issued, authorizing local enterprises to retain, for development purposes, surplus profits obtained from the sale of their products and to make other readjustments in programmes of capital development already authorized, without reference to the central Government, provided these did not involve an increase in the total funds used.

It will be seen that these changes were as sweeping in their effect as the Khrushchev reorganization in Russia. They were, however, by no means a mere imitation of the new Soviet system. In China a larger proportion of the economy, including most of heavy industry, seems to have been retained under the centralized control of the industrial ministries; and no single regional economic authority has been set up having economic powers comparable to the Soviet Sovnarkhozy. There are three effective economic tiers, instead of two as in Russia. Thus the new system in China does not yet seem to attempt to serve the main purpose aimed at by the Khrushchev system, that is the breaking down of the huge autarkic and uneconomic vertical combines built up by the industrial ministries in Moscow. This does not appear to have been regarded by the Chinese Government as representing a serious danger in China. On the other hand the Chinese authorities do seem to have wished to bring about a much greater degree of genuine decentralization in the fields which have been freed, principally light industry, commerce, and construction, delegating considerably increased powers both to the local authorities and to the individual enterprises. Thus, while both Governments had clearly become convinced of the clumsiness and inflexibility of a rigidly centralized bureaucratic system of industrial control, the remedies that were introduced in the two countries differ widely. It may be interesting to see how the two systems fare, and how far either may come to be modified to bring it nearer to the other.

Related to this development an increasing stress was laid by the Chinese leaders at this time on the importance of small-scale production. In the drive to increase production of coal and iron, many small-scale mines were developed or reopened, and there were repeated calls to the industrial ministries and local authorities not to neglect the possibilities of small enterprises in every field. In the spring of 1957 Li Fu-chun said:

> We cannot demand that all factories, mines and enterprises are equipped with modernised equipment. . . . We must first consider before plunging into modernisation and automation. At present we are doing just the opposite; some factories which need not be modernised are being modernised and thus much waste takes place. . . . In general, enterprises both under the Central Government and local governments, should be medium or small in size and the few large enterprises should be integrated with these.[1]

In construction work there should be less mechanization, and more should be done by hand. One advantage of this system was that it would enable China to be more independent of outside, i.e. Russian, aid. 'If the construction scale and standards are lowered we will be able to construct more of our own factories and mines. We should do our best to accomplish things with our own efforts.'[2]

Proposals for the second Five-Year Plan due to begin in 1958 were drawn up by the 1956 Congress of the CCP.[3] These suggested that the total value of industrial and agricultural production in 1962 should be about 75 per cent. higher than the target originally planned for 1957, as against the increase of 51·1 per cent. originally planned in the first Five-Year Plan, which was then likely to be over-fulfilled by nearly 10 per cent. (in fact, it was announced at the end of 1957 that the first Five-Year Plan had been over-fulfilled by 17 per cent.). In practice, therefore, what was called for was an increase of just under 65 per cent., as against an expected increase of about 60 per cent. achieved in the first Five-Year Plan. The output of capital goods was to be developed faster than the output of consumer goods, so that by 1962 each should represent about 50 per cent. of the volume of industrial output, as against

[1] Li Fu-chun in a speech to a conference of cadres, *NCNA*, 27 May 1957.
[2] Ibid.   [3] *Proposals for Second Five-Year Plan.*

proportions of 38 per cent. and 62 per cent. respectively planned for 1957. It was hoped that the national income would increase by about 50 per cent. during the course of the Plan. Expenditure on defence and administration was to be cut down, reducing the proportion of expenditure under these two headings together to 20 per cent. of budget expenditure, as against 32 per cent. for 1957, and allowing expenditure on 'economic construction and cultural development' to rise from 56 per cent. to 60–70 per cent. As a result state investment in capital construction might be about double what it was during the first Five-Year Plan. The proportion of this sum going to industry and agriculture would be increased to 60 per cent. and 10 per cent. respectively (from 58·2 and 7·6 per cent.) of the total, leaving 30 per cent. for capital development in communications, trade, banking, administration, &c.

The CCP resolution proposed that by 1962 the production of electricity should reach 40–43 million kwh., of coal 190–210 million tons, of steel 10·5–12 million tons, and of crude oil 5–6 million tons. In the field of agriculture a total output of about 275 million tons of grain and of about 2·4 million tons of cotton was aimed at. Production of some of the principal consumer goods was to be about doubled. Other ambitious targets were set in many fields.

Before the Plan started, however, there were various signs that the Government were having second thoughts about various aspects of the Plan targets originally proposed. Although the second Five-Year Plan was due to begin in 1958, by the end of 1957 no definitive targets had been adopted. In particular, the Chinese leaders may have been considering some readjustment in the balance to be maintained between the development to be given to heavy industry on the one hand and to agricultural and consumer-goods production on the other. Many of the Chinese leaders seem to have drawn the conclusion that the unhappy experiences of 1956 had proved the disastrous effect of aiming at too high a rate of expansion for heavy industry without balancing this with a corresponding development of agriculture and consumer-goods industries in order to mop up the surplus purchasing power created. At a conference of design experts at the beginning of June 1957, Po I-po and Li Fu-chun said that one of the essential tasks of the Plan was to ensure a balance between capital accumulation and consumption, to ensure increasing consumption, a steady improvement in living standards, and a stable market. Among other things this would provide a bigger market and so more capital for the state.[1] In August Po I-po announced that the major 'contradiction' in the economy at that time was that the production of consumer goods was lagging behind the development of the economy as a whole, while, at the same time, the development of the raw-materials industries was lagging behind that of the processing and manufacturing industries. It was thus, he considered, vitally important during the second Five-Year Plan to give the maximum possible emphasis to the development of agriculture and the raw-materials industries, such as coal mining and the oil industry.[2]

By the time the new plan started at the beginning of 1958, however, any misgivings that may have been felt in some quarters about the wisdom of resuming a break-neck rate of industrial development seem to have been brushed aside. At about that time a new slogan was put out demanding that China should catch up with, or surpass, British output of steel and other major industrial products within fifteen years, i.e. by 1972, by which time Chinese steel output should reach 40 million tons a year. At the meeting of the National People's Congress at the beginning of February a call was made for a 'Great Leap Forward' in economic development during the next three years. Demands for an increase of 19 per cent. in the production of steel, 18 per cent. in the production of electricity, 17 per cent. in coal production in 1958, and corresponding increases in other industries were published. Li Hsien-nien stated that 'incorrect judgements had at one time been made on some of the financial and economic problems that arose in the winter of 1956, such as the overspending on invest-ment',[3] but claimed that all such conservative forces had now been overcome and the way prepared for another period of rapid expansion.

During the next few months the campaign for a Great Leap Forward was waged with the greatest intensity throughout the

[1] *NCNA*, 7 June 1957.   [2] *JMJP*, 10 Aug. 1957.   [3] Ibid., 12 Feb. 1957.

country. Workers in every kind of enterprise, in the factories, on the railways, in the shops, and on the farms pledged themselves to achieve startling improvements in their previous performances and were said to have demanded that their output targets for 1958 should be raised. In the countryside many local authorities undertook to achieve the 1967 production targets during 1958. The national targets for all the major products were raised, some of them several times in succession. The steel target was raised from 6·2 million tons in February, to 7 million tons in March, to 8–8·5 million tons in May, and finally, after a special meeting of the Political Bureau, to 10·7 million tons, about double the previous year's production, in August. Other targets were little less ambitious. Already, on 20 March, the *New China News Agency* was able to forecast that Chinese industrial production might increase by 33 per cent. during 1958, instead of 14·6 per cent. as planned by the National People's Congress only a month and a half earlier.

There were especially big increases in the targets for local-authority-controlled industry. Local authorities were to make it their aim to raise the value of their industrial production to equal that of their agricultural production within the next few years. Large numbers of small and medium-sized low-cost factories and mines were to be built by the county authorities and agricultural co-operatives. Standard designs for these were worked out by the central ministries, and cadres for the provinces were called to Peking for special courses of instruction in building methods. Sometimes state factories gave assistance to the local authorities in establishing these local plants. They trained the management staff and gave advice over construction and production methods. Large towns often entered into special arrangements with the new factories in the surrounding areas, for example by undertaking construction work, supplying raw materials, or entering into agreements to purchase some of the finished products. Agreements between provinces were also made. In 1958 an agreement was reached between Szechwan, Yunnan, Kweichow, and Shensi, under which the relatively advanced province of Szechwan was to provide technical aid and industrial equipment in exchange for mining equipment and materials. The province of Heilungkiang offered to give help to other provinces, especially for heavy industry.

Gradually there was a shift of emphasis on to the very smallest scale plants. Publicity was given to the plans of the rural authorities and individual farms for the construction of tiny iron-casting furnaces of anything down to 1·5 cu.m. capacity, capable of producing 500 tons of iron a year at a cost of less than 100 yuan (about £15) a ton. The importance of making use of native-type furnaces using traditional methods was repeatedly emphasized. Besides the iron foundries, small-scale 'fertilizer factories', coal, iron, and lead mines, instrument repair shops and plants for the manufacture of ball-bearings were the projects most widely undertaken. Some idea of the scale of some of these establishments can be gauged from the fact that in a single province, Hopei, there were said to be 500,000 such 'factories and workshops' by the end of June, while Chekiang was reported to have set up 300,000 between April and June. It is clear that in many cases small blacksmiths' furnaces and sheds used for repairing tools, or collections of manure and compost, were being dignified by the name of 'factories' or 'fertilizer plants'.

In August 1958 the Peking radio and press announced a new movement, said to have already become widespread in some provinces, for the establishment of 'People's Public Associations', usually translated into English as 'People's Communes'. The movement was said to have started in Honan in April and later to have spread to other provinces. It took the form of the merging of about 20 or 30 co-operatives including 20,000 or more members, spread over forty to a hundred villages, into single communes, independent administrative and economic units, having control of all the means of production and the entire labour force within its area. The new unit was said to provide 'unified management' of industry, agriculture, commerce, education, and military affairs. Payment of all members, both industrial and agricultural, was partly by wage payments and partly by the system of 'free supply', under which members obtained some of their food, housing, clothing, and other necessities without payment. Communal dining-rooms and nurseries were widely set up.

The communes thus became responsible for the running of all the small-scale industrial projects formerly under the control of the individual co-operatives or of the *hsiang*, previously the smallest unit of local government. Indeed, it seems possible that, although ideological grounds could be brought forward in support of the new system, which was held up as an important advance on the road to Communism, the basic reason for their establishment at this time was an economic one. Early reports of the mergers said that they had taken place 'because of the increasing demands of industrial construction, the need for improving the members' livelihood further and to solve other problems involving manpower and materials'. It was claimed that the old co-operatives had proved themselves too small to control the activities of the newly established local industry, to undertake the irrigation works that were then being carried out all over the countryside, or to provide and allocate the investment funds necessary for these tasks. The provision of communal kitchens, dining halls, and nurseries (which were widely set up in the big towns as well), though it could be represented as a step in the direction of a communist society, was, at bottom, designed to free women for work in the fields, so releasing men for work in the mines, blast furnaces, and repair shops. It seems that, as in other instances, the Chinese Government, rather than determining their policies in order to conform with ideological precept, set up the new social forms in response to immediate practical requirements, and only later devised the ideological arguments to justify them.

The new communes thus became the focus for the drive to set up the new, tiny, and usually antiquated, 'industrial' undertakings. One commune, which became a model for those set up all over the country, was said to have established over 1,000 small factories, while another was reported to have set up in a few weeks 4,500 'iron and steel, machine-building, chemical fertilizer and other plants' (it must be remembered that an average commune contained about 5,000 households). By October 600,000 small blast furnaces were reported to have been set up all over the country. An intense campaign was waged to mobilize the members of the communes to help reach the target of 10·7 million tons of steel demanded by the Political Bureau. University students, writers and artists, Communist

Party officials and housewives were all called on to contribute by themselves participating in factory and commune.

It seems doubtful whether in many cases the iron and steel produced by these methods was of a form or quality that was of much value for manufacturing purposes: articles in the press sought to overcome doubts which, it was admitted, many in China felt about the value of the native-type iron and steel products. At the same time serious bottlenecks in communications seem to have resulted from the effort to transport the products of innumerable local furnaces dotted about all over the country. Towards the end of the year it seems that the authorities themselves had become convinced of the necessity for a change in the programme. It was announced that thousands of the local-type metal-smelting furnaces were being amalgamated and mechanized. The aim was to concentrate the local production of iron and steel in 600–1,000 iron and steel centres all over China. These would be situated as near as possible to supplies of raw materials and would, it was hoped, produce up to 20,000 tons of steel a year each. During this process the best types of furnaces would be selected and the rest eliminated: in other words hundreds of thousands of the small furnaces that had just been set up, or resuscitated, with such enthusiasm over the whole country, were now to be abandoned. On 1 April 1960, Li Fu-chun revealed that there were then only about 1,300 'small' iron-smelting enterprises of modern type in the whole country, of which about 200 would be developed into 'medium-sized or small iron and steel complexes'.

At the end of the year grandiloquent claims were made for the achievements of the first year of the Great Leap Forward. It was announced that industrial production in 1958 had been 65 per cent. higher than in 1957. The output of machine tools had been trebled, the production of coal and steel doubled, production of oil increased by more than 50 per cent. and of electricity by 40 per cent. Other claims were not much less startling. Some of these claims were almost certainly highly exaggerated. It certainly seems that during 1958 the statistical procedures employed in China underwent a significant relaxation. Faith in the published figures was not strengthened by such claims as that production of iron in October 1958 was 440 per cent., and of coal 190 per cent., higher than in the previous month; or by the sudden rise in the estimate for China's iron deposits, following the mobilization of the peasantry in seeking out new deposits, from 11,000 million tons at the end of 1957 to 100,000 million tons by the end of 1958. It seems certain that, whatever may have been the case in previous years, when the published figures, though striking, were not beyond belief, during 1958 the figures published were not obtained by any system of central inspection, or from the estimates of purchasing or transport agencies, but simply by adding the enthusiastic claims of ambitious local officials, faced with the need to vie with their neighbours in fulfilling intimidating production targets. That such a procedure did not always provide reliable statistical information was implicitly confirmed by subsequent admissions of the Government.

Even when all allowances are made, however, it seems likely that there did occur during 1958 a very considerable rise in industrial production. This was partly obtained by a large increase in the output of locally controlled industry, often on a doll's house scale, to which the Government had increasingly turned to bring about the increases in production, especially of iron and steel, which they were hoping for. These undertakings were often so small in scale and old-fashioned in method that they would never have been considered economic propositions in developed countries. But for a country such as China, short of capital but rich in labour, they may well, at least temporarily, have served an important function.

Nevertheless it is clear that during the early part of 1959 there was some rethinking about the form the Great Leap Forward should take; and of the function that the communes should play within this. The organization and structure of the communes was overhauled (see below, p. 165). The failure of the small-scale iron-smelting plants had shown that the value of communes for most industrial purposes was limited. There was increasing talk of 'realism', 'economy', 'planning', 'more down-to-earth target-setting'. Still greater emphasis was to be given to agricultural production. Chou En-lai said that 80 per cent. of the Chinese labour force should take part in agriculture, and that state factories must cease to recruit labour in the countryside. Commune production was to be increasingly geared to purely agricultural activities, the repair of machinery, the preparation of fertilizers, and the production of some handicraft goods for local consumption. And even within the communes a larger proportion of the labour force was to be concentrated in purely agricultural activities.

There were other efforts to improve the efficiency of the system. It was admitted that during 1958 the transport system had proved inadequate to dispose of the products of commune industry which had accumulated in remote rural areas, badly served by communications. This was certainly one of the reasons for concentrating iron and steel production and using commune industry mainly to serve local needs. Later in 1959 there were intensive efforts to develop local transportation services. The *People's Daily* said in December that transport had become the key to the successful fulfilment of the production plans for 1959 and 1960. It was admitted that, for example, 13 million tons of coal was piled up within 30 km. of railway lines waiting to be transported to the railhead; 10 million people were said to be working in local communications, many with 'nothing but their hands and their shoulders'. There was to be a development of all forms of local transport from carts and shoulder-poles to local native-type railways, with rails made of cast-iron, or timber covered with sheet-iron, and locomotives powered by gas, diesel, or automobile engines. 'In such a country as ours, all means of transport, whether foreign or native, are useful and should be permitted', the *People's Daily* declared. 'Carts, wooden railways and cable-ways should be popularized.'

It is quite clear that because of difficulties of this sort there was widespread criticism at this period, both within the Communist Party and without, of the whole policy of the Great Leap Forward and of commune-run industry. Some people, it was later admitted, regarded this programme as 'petty-bourgeois fanaticism', and the communes as a 'mess'. The former industrial bourgeoisie appeared to have been particularly sceptical. Such critics stated, it was said, that the movement cost too much, produced poor goods, and squeezed out more important things. Such doubts must have been intensified by the shortages of food which occurred at this time, belying the widely publicized claims of a gigantic harvest the previous summer, and the evident uselessness of commune iron and steel for industrial purposes.

It was no doubt because of this mounting disillusion that, in August 1959, the Central Committee were obliged to admit that many of the claims made at the end of the previous year were exaggerated and that in consequence the targets for the current year had also been set far too high. Besides substantial reductions in the agricultural claims for 1958, it was admitted that of the 11 million tons of steel produced that year, that part, 3 million tons, produced by the backyard methods was not of a quality to 'meet the requirements of industry' and such products would no longer be included in the figures of steel production. The steel target for 1959 went down from 18 million tons to 12 million, coal from 380 to 335 million tons. The original targets for the Second Plan, previously considered as too conservative, were re-adopted.

The sharp campaign that was initiated at the same time against rightists who expressed criticism or pessimism about the policy of the Great Leap Forward was no doubt made necessary by the fact that such criticisms had now been demonstrated as to some extent justified. But more than anything the leadership feared the sceptical attitude of mind that lay behind these criticisms. For such people, it was said, 'attack doctrinairism but mean Marxism'. The régime were willing to accept some of the practical adjustments implicit in the criticisms, but not the basic attitude underlying them. Enthusiasm remained obligatory.

Red Flag denied that the balance of the economy had been upset by the Big Leap even if there had been local and temporary lack of co-ordination. However, from this time there were intense efforts to prevent individual communes from trying to develop an entirely autarkic economy within their own area, so reverting to the virtual self-sufficiency of traditional Chinese agricultural society. Among other things such policies deprived the state of the taxes it received from trade in commodities for sale. The popular slogan became 'Make the whole country into one chess-board', that is a single interdependent economic area. Fairs were organized to promote exchanges between communes. A national fair was held at Canton (in addition to the export fair held in the same city) to promote exchanges between the large cities such as Shanghai, Canton, and Peking, supplying manufactured goods, hardware, electricity and agricultural machinery to the peasants in exchange for agricultural products. In September 1959 a directive was published to allow municipalities to have jurisdiction over the country areas in the immediate vicinity, to 'promote mutual support between industry and agriculture'. There were further efforts to improve communications facilities. There was to be increasing co-operation between the big state factories and the communes in the surrounding countryside, which would receive technical assistance in return for doing processing or repair work for the factories. Co-ordination became the reaction to the disruption created in the initial stages by the new system.

In view of the now chastened state of mind of the leaders, it is perhaps not surprising that the results claimed for 1959 were not quite so implausible as those announced a year before. None the less production of steel was said to have increased by 67 per cent. over the previous year, of coal by 29 per cent., with other increases ranging from about 15 per cent. (in cotton cloth) to about 65 per cent. (for oil). The new figures were themselves sufficiently striking. A number of the results claimed were higher than those originally aimed at in the final year of the plan.

For this reason there may still have been some scepticism about the figures. At any rate the campaign against the doubters continued to be waged with intensity. At the beginning of 1960 there occurred a two-month-long joint session of the Chinese Democratic National Construction Association and the All-China Federation of Industry and Commerce, the organizations of ex-business men designed to promote the campaign for remoulding the industrial and commercial classes. At the end of the meeting a message of respect was sent to Mao Tse-tung, obediently pledging 'whole-hearted obedience, whole-hearted acceptance of socialist transformation, whole-hearted service to socialism'. But on 1 March the *People's Daily*, commenting on the meeting, said that though the industrialists and business men had made progress,

a majority of them are sceptical and wavering in their acceptance of the Communist party's leadership, towards the general line, the Great Leap Forward and the people's communes. Some of them are dissatisfied or even opposed to these things. . . . It would take a long time to transform their bourgeois attitudes and substitute proletarian ones.

The leaders themselves had certainly not lost their faith in the efficiency of a violent forward movement, even if by primitive methods, nor in the commune as the unit most effective in achieving this. During the first half of 1960 the introduction of communes in the towns, temporarily halted at the end of 1958, because 'bourgeois prejudices remained prevalent among many of the capitalists and intellectuals in the cities', was resumed. References in the press made it clear that in fact throughout 1959 experiments with urban communes were being made in a number of towns, in particular Chengchow and other cities in Honan. It was later reported that 'even in the experimental year of 1959' so-called 'neighbourhood industries' in Peking, Shanghai, Tientsin, Wuhan, and Canton, had engaged in production and processing work worth 800 million yuan. By November 1959 200,000 Peking housewives were said to be working in 590 neighbourhood workshops under the guidance of local Communist Party organizations. On 30 March 1960 Li Fu-chun announced that the development of urban communes was then to be carried out on a large scale. The secretaries of the municipal committees of the Communist Party in Peking, Shanghai, Tientsin, Wuhan, and Canton announced that these cities would set up people's communes throughout their area by stages—though at the same time membership would be by 'voluntary participation' only. The urban communes quite often include outlying rural areas, where agriculture is practised, as well as parts of towns. In one, in the suburbs of Peking, 14 per cent. of the population are peasants and the rest urban workers of one sort or another.

The city communes are said to be able to 'organize and arrange the urban labour force in a unified and rational way,

gradually organize all the people in the city able to work, and
so turn consumers into producers'. The main advantage, as in
the country, is that the provision of communal dining-rooms
enables housewives to take up other work. The workers made
available work for state, as well as commune, enterprises. Most
of the communes' own undertakings, like those in the country,
are on a rudimentary scale. In one commune at Harbin it was
said that 'hundreds of small workshops run by the neighbour-
hoods had been processing parts and accessories for the big
state-owned factories, and using scrap material to turn out
small articles for daily use'. Administrative services provided
by the communes are said to include, besides the communal
dining-rooms, nurseries, and kindergartens, schools, libraries,
recreational activities, laundries, clothes mending, house
cleaning, decorating, hairdressing, and the repair of bicycles,
furniture, and other articles. But there is no doubt that this
gives a quite inflated picture of the organization in an average
commune.

There have been careful assurances that all personal be-
longings of the commune members will remain their own
property. In some cases responsibility in certain fields is being
taken over by the communes from the existing municipal
authorities. It may be that in the long run urban communes
will become autonomous administrative and economic units,
roughly corresponding to the existing *ch'u* or wards. But for
the moment, the *People's Daily* has said, the urban communes
should be 'diverse in form to suit the complex conditions in the
cities'. It is thus too soon to predict their final form.

Meanwhile the emphasis was being shifted still further in
favour of agriculture. Li Fu-chun said at the beginning of 1960
that agriculture was to be 'the foundation' (a phrase echoing
Confucian belief throughout the centuries), while industry was
to be 'the leading factor'. Throughout 1959 many town-
dwellers continued to be sent out to help with irrigation work,
with harvesting and with countering disasters in the countryside. The changed emphasis was reflected in the 1960 budget.
This provided for expenditure on economic construction 33 per
cent. higher than the previous year, and expenditure on social
services 47 per cent. higher. But the investment funds of the

communes were to be increased by 50 per cent., rising to about 1,500 million yuan (£217 million), while capital investment in agriculture, including related sectors, was to increase by 63 per cent. to 3,910 yuan (about £566 million). An increasing share of industrial production was to be allocated to agricultural needs. More steel was to be given to the production of agricultural machinery. The first tractor factory at Loyang, having a capacity of 15,000 caterpillar tractors a year, went into operation in November 1959.

At the same time there was continuing emphasis on the importance of technical innovation, both within the communes, where much still depended on getting the best possible value from antiquated implements, and in the small-scale iron mines and steel mills, where it was hoped to obtain useful additions to production without the very latest Soviet-built equipment. Maximum publicity was given to every feat of improvisation by the peasants of the communes to improve the working of existing equipment or to devise new forms. Meanwhile the pace remained a hot one. The slogan was still 'Go all out, aim high and get more, quicker, better and more economical results to build socialism.'

The whole philosophy of the leaders at this period was summed up in the slogan 'walking on two feet'. This meant that there must be efforts to develop, at the same time, not only the most modern up-to-date industrial methods developed in the West, but also many traditional Chinese techniques which could be much more cheaply exploited until modern equipment could be provided (this included, for example, the resuscitation of Chinese native medicine, herbs and acupuncture, so utilizing those already skilled in these techniques while others were being trained in Western medicine); not only heavy industry, but light industry and agriculture; not only huge industrial undertakings run by the state, but the small dispersed plants developed by the local authorities and the communes.

However, the hopes that had been placed on achievement in the final year of the Great Leap Forward were disappointed by the extremely bad harvest during 1960, the disruption caused by floods, typhoons, and other natural calamities (some mines and factories in Manchuria were put out of action by floods), and the diversion of some labour to help in agricultural tasks. As a result, though by the end of 1960 many of the targets for heavy industry had been reached, others for light industry and agriculture, whose products were more important for improving the standard of living (and whose production levels could, too, most easily be ascertained by the ordinary population), were not achieved. The events of that year made the Chinese leaders more conscious than ever that their ambitious aims in the field of industrial development were dependent for their fulfilment on the satisfactory solution of those more humdrum, but more basic, problems that had afflicted governments of China for hundreds of years before them.

A new mood, less wildly ambitious, more sober and practical, crept into the direction of the economy. The immediate aim was to be retrenchment. Quality became more important than quantity. It at last began to be recognized that the transformation of China from poverty to prosperity could not be achieved with quite the lightning rapidity once hoped. The new China was not to be built in a day.

VII

SOVIET AID

SOVIET assistance was a vital factor in Chinese development during the first Five-Year Plan. This help did not consist of free grants-in-aid. It took the form of loans bearing a low rate of interest, or of industrial exports which are repaid mainly by Chinese deliveries of agricultural and mineral products. In addition, the Chinese enjoyed the benefit of Soviet advice and assistance in the preparation of their industrialization plans. And a large army of Soviet advisers and technicians have played an essential part in the execution of these plans.

The original basis for Sino-Soviet economic co-operation was set out in the economic agreement which was signed at the same time as the Treaty of Friendship, Alliance, and Mutual Assistance in February 1950. This provided for a Soviet loan to China of $300 million at 1 per cent. per annum over a five-year period for the purchase of Soviet materials and equipment. The loan fell far short of Chinese needs, and the length of time taken over the negotiations for the treaty suggests that there was some fairly hard bargaining over its terms.

In 1953, with the launching of the Five-Year Plan, further arrangements, providing for increased Soviet assistance, were made. In March agreements were reached providing for Soviet aid in building or expanding electric-power plants in China and in the supply of equipment for agriculture, the mining, machine-building, metallurgical, chemical, and power industries, and for transport; China was to export in return agricultural products and non-ferrous metals. In September, as the result of further and apparently prolonged negotiations, a new agreement was reached providing for Soviet aid in the construction or rebuilding during the period 1950–9 of 141 large-scale industrial plants. This represented the main Soviet effort in assisting China to launch her first Five-Year Plan. Of the 141 plants 91 were to be new factories, and the remainder reconstructed or renovated plants. The arrangements provided for

Soviet assistance in siting and planning factories, in the provision of new equipment, in the supply of technicians by the Soviet Union, and in the training of Chinese technicians in Soviet methods.

The 141 enterprises included modern iron and steel complexes, non-ferrous metallurgical plants, coal mines, oil refineries, power stations, chemical works, and factories of many sorts. They thus represented some of the key enterprises of the future Chinese economy, and were to enable China to produce out of domestic resources motor vehicles, locomotives, tractors, and aeroplanes. Most of the enterprises would be completed by 1959, but some would take up to ten years to complete. Seventeen were in fact wholly or partially built in the course of 1953, and were put into operation in 1954. By the end of the first Five-Year Plan, fifty-seven were said to have been completed.

In October 1954 a further measure of Soviet aid was announced. The new agreement provided for a loan of 520 million roubles (about £45 million at the official rate of exchange, though less in real terms) and an increase in exports of capital equipment of 400 million roubles to cover supplementary aid for the 141 plants and assistance in constructing 15 new ones. It was later announced that the equipment supplied by the Soviet Union for the 156 enterprises and for 21 other machine shops covered by other agreements was worth about 5,600 million roubles, or about £400 million at the official rate of exchange.

On 4 January 1956 it was announced that a comprehensive programme for scientific and technical co-operation had been worked out at the third meeting of the Sino-Soviet Commission in December 1955. Under its terms the Soviet Union was to supply China with designs for non-ferrous metallurgical plants, for the coal industry and for the construction of railways, and with blueprints of equipment for blast furnaces and various types of machinery. China was to send experts to the Soviet Union to study her metallurgical, coal, oil, and textile industries, while the Soviet Union would in return send experts to China to study the cultivation of various crops and other subjects.

In April 1956 two further agreements were reached. The first provided for the construction of 55 new plants in addition to the 156 plants already being built with Soviet aid. Among the 55 were metallurgical, machine-building, and chemical plants, factories producing synthetic fibre and plastics, synthetic and liquid fuel, power stations, and scientific research institutions for the aeronautical industry. The total value of the equipment to be supplied, the designing work and other kinds of technical assistance provided by the Soviet Union for building the plants was put at about 2,500 million roubles (about £230 million at the official rate of exchange). According to the communiqué the Chinese Government will repay this sum through trade deliveries.[1] It appeared that these plants were not in fact to be built until the second Five-Year Plan beginning in 1958. The other agreement contained arrangements for co-ordinating the building of the railway across Sinkiang from Lanchow in Kansu to Aktogai in Soviet Turkestan, and for the organization of a through-traffic service on this railway by 1960.

In August 1958 a further agreement was signed in Moscow under which the Soviet Union was to give technical assistance in the construction or expansion of another forty-seven industrial projects. These differed from those covered in earlier agreements in that most of them could be surveyed and designed by the Chinese, and the Russians would merely supply the basic equipment. For the others, Russian experts would be sent to plan and advise as under previous agreements. Finally, on 7 February 1959, it was announced that yet another agreement had been signed between the two countries. Under this the Soviet Union was to provide aid worth 5,000 million roubles (about £446 million at the official rate of exchange). The programme was to cover eight years and would provide for the building of seventy-eight big metallurgical, coal, oil, and other enterprises.

The terms governing the receipt and application of Soviet financial and technical aid are set out in the report of the Committee of Financial and Economic Affairs which was approved at the 26th session of the State Administrative

---

[1] This is probably the explanation of the fact that in recent years China appears to have had a substantial trading surplus with the Soviet Union.

Council on 15 September 1953. This report was made at the time of the first major instalment of Soviet aid, the agreement to build or rebuild the 141 industrial plants. The announcement said that such aid was to cover the selection of premises and collection of basic materials for planning, determination of procedure for planning, the planning operation itself, the supply of equipment, guidance in the construction, installation, and operation of machinery and free provision of 'technical know-how'; and the provision of this technical knowledge was to continue while the new production processes were being learnt. The agreement also included provision for an annual intake into Soviet enterprises of Chinese workers and engineering personnel for field training, as well as for assistance to be given by Soviet experts in existing Chinese enterprises.

Soviet advisers and technicians permeate almost every branch of Chinese industry. But in some fields this influence is particularly marked. The work of prospecting for minerals and the general development of the mining industries, for example, appears to be heavily dependent on Soviet material and technical assistance. The Soviet Union is the main consumer of the non-ferrous metals produced in China, and has had a traditional interest in the exploitation of mineral resources in Sinkiang. Soviet advisers have been particularly numerous in the North East, where a large proportion of the plants being built with Soviet aid are situated. In many such enterprises the technical direction must have been almost entirely in Soviet hands in the early stages of the Plan, though there is little doubt that the Chinese take over complete control as soon as they are competent to do so.

The Chinese have imitated some Soviet methods in the fields of government administration and economic organization, for example in the system of local government, the use of Five-Year Plans, the planning mechanism, the specialized economic ministries, and the structure and functions of the Communist Party.

Soviet influence is also strong in the field of higher education. The Chinese Five-Year Plan calls for the training of 650,000–700,000 additional 'technical-managerial' personnel. To meet this demand a reorganization of Chinese higher educational institutions has taken place, amounting to an adoption of the Soviet system of centralized higher education, i.e. the establishment of general universities and of technical institutes of engineering, mining, geology, agriculture, medicine, teachers' training, economics, and finance. Many Soviet textbooks are in use, and Russian is widely taught in the schools though there has recently been a movement for the reintroduction of English. Many Chinese students receive higher education in the Soviet Union and other Communist countries.

In one respect China has become more independent in her economic relations with the Soviet Union over the last few years. Soon after the régime was established various joint Sino-Soviet mixed companies, similar to those set up in Eastern Europe, were formed for the purpose of exploiting particular sections of the Chinese economy in which Russia had a traditional interest. The object was presumably that the Soviet Union should supply skilled techniques and equipment to help run the various enterprises, and would gain in return some measure of control over the enterprises and the use to which their products were put. The principal Sino-Soviet companies were concerned with the exploitation of mineral and petroleum resources in Sinkiang, the running of air transport in Sinkiang and on other routes to the Soviet Union, and shipbuilding in Dairen (of which the port is still under Soviet control). Under agreements reached in October 1954 all these companies were handed back to sole Chinese control.

Great care has been taken to keep the army of Soviet technicians and advisers as far as possible out of contact with the traditionally xenophobic Chinese people. There has been a spate of propaganda designed to publicize the benefits received from this aid and to acclaim the generosity of the Soviet Union. This has, however, not always been successful. For example, in a speech to the National People's Congress in June 1957[1] Chou En-lai revealed that 'some people are against learning from the experience of the Soviet Union and even say that the mistakes and shortcomings in our construction work are also the result of learning from the Soviet Union'.

There were a good many signs that the Chinese leaders themselves would not be sorry to acquire a greater degree of

[1] BBC, Suppl. No. 1, 28 June 1957, p. 12.

independence from their Soviet benefactors as soon as they could do this without serious embarrassment to their development plans. During the last year or two there have been a number of announcements underlining what Chinese native designers and engineers were able to achieve independently of any outside assistance. It was said, for example, that China could already design without help many types of factories and machinery for which formerly Soviet assistance had been necessary. It was announced in 1957 that, by the end of the second Five-Year Plan in 1962, China would produce at least 70 per cent. of her own machinery, as against 40 per cent. during the first Five-Year Plan. And there was almost a note of triumph in the announcement that the Soviet experts at the No. 1 Car Works at Changchun had gone home and that its future production, including that of six-seater cars, would be designed entirely by Chinese.

In his budget speech in July 1957 Li Hsien-nien, the Minister of Finance, said that, since the founding of the People's Republic, Soviet aid amounted to 5,294 million yuan (about £750 million). This amount, though substantial, is not huge in relation to China's needs when it is considered that no other source of external aid is open to her at present. It compares with a total of £350 million and £600 million of external aid provided for in the first and second Five-Year Plans of India, a country with only three-quarters of the population of China and starting from a more advanced base. Moreover the flow of funds from Russia to China is not likely to be maintained at this level. In the same speech Li Hsien-nien said that the total receipts in foreign loans in 1957 would be only 23 million yuan (about £3·5 million): China was now in a better position to rely on her own accumulation to carry on national construction, he claimed. The agreements of 1958 and 1959 have now somewhat altered the position. But it may well be that the flow of funds from the Soviet Union will soon begin to decline, and that the Chinese leaders will not be able to expect aid in the future on the scale they have had so far.

Under the agreement of 1950 repayments of the Soviet $300 million credit were supposed to begin in 1954 (at the rate of $30 million a year), and these have presumably now started.

It was announced in the agreement that 'in view of the extreme devastation of China as a result of prolonged hostilities on its territory, the Soviet Government has agreed to grant credits on favourable terms of 1% annual interest'. Since no announcement was made about the terms of repayment of other assistance subsequently granted by the Soviet Union, these may well be less favourable to China, and the payments will presumably in time represent something of a burden on her slender resources: in 1958 China was running a trade surplus of £100 million.

Even if the rate of interest paid by the Chinese is in fact low, the prices paid for Chinese raw materials by Russia are believed to be unfavourable. In any event the Chinese, having only recently emerged from dependence on the West in the industrial field, no doubt continue to be irked by the acute dependence on the Soviet Union which has succeeded it. By their practice of agreeing only to finance the construction of specific enterprises in China rather than making available credits which might be spent as the Chinese planners themselves chose, and by the widespread penetration of Chinese planning bureaux by Soviet advisers and technicians, the Soviet Union clearly has had a considerable influence over the development of the first Chinese Five-Year Plan, and indeed over the direction and methods of Chinese industrialization in general.[1]

The extent of China's dependence on the Soviet Union was demonstrated by the authenticated reports that, during the ideological dispute between the two countries during the summer of 1960, the Soviet technicians in China were abruptly withdrawn *en masse* to the Soviet Union. This must have revealed to the Chinese leaders, in the most powerful form, how far, if she wishes to continue to enjoy the benefits of Soviet technical assistance—and there seems nowhere else for her to turn for this at the moment—she may be obliged, in the final resort, to conform with Soviet wishes in other fields.

It is not easy to judge how far differences of opinion may have

[1] Dependence on the Soviet Union and shortage of capital have not, however, prevented the Chinese Government from themselves entering into agreements, providing for Chinese aid, for example, to North Korea, Mongolia, North Vietnam, Indonesia, the Yemen, Cambodia, and Nepal.

arisen behind the scenes over the uses to which the Soviet assistance should be put, and how far the Soviet Union may have made use of her monopoly position as a supplier of aid, to direct Chinese industrial expansion in directions other than those desired by the Chinese themselves—official communications naturally speak of nothing but single-minded agreement and heartfelt Chinese gratitude for the generosity of their benefactors. On the whole, the programme does not seem very different from what a backward but rapidly developing power might be expected to embark on. But the Chinese must be keenly conscious of the commanding position occupied by the Soviet Union within their economy, and will no doubt in the long run, welcome the prospect of some alternative source of capital to increase their bargaining power, especially over prices. Nevertheless, although in their present mood they would be very unlikely to accept aid from the United States.

Without any supply of external capital, however, the expansion of the Chinese economy would clearly have been very much slower. The Chinese Government are thus obliged to take what help they can get. Certainly no alternative source of capital seems likely to be available to them within the foreseeable future, and the realization of their industrial aims will therefore probably remain for a considerable time partly dependent on the goodwill of the Soviet Union. This must certainly be an important factor in the conduct of their ideological dispute with the Soviet Union. They must be conscious that the rate of economic progress that will be achieved by China and Albania, the two most under-developed countries of the Communist world, if they were to remain alone together in isolation, would be a very slow one. They must be acutely conscious that there might be very great material benefit in some sacrifice of theoretical rectitude. Ideological purity being prized as it is by Communists, however, it would be foolish to be sure that prosperity will necessarily be preferred to principle.

THE TRANSFORMATION OF THE
ECONOMIC FRAMEWORK

VIII

THE TREATMENT OF PRIVATE ENTERPRISE

In 'On Coalition Government' published in 1945, Mao Tse-tung wrote: 'The task of our New Democratic system is . . . to promote the free development of a private capitalist economy that benefits instead of controlling the people's livelihood, and to protect all honestly acquired private property.'[1] Even after they came to power, the Chinese communists were still aware of the need for injecting confidence into the privately owned sector of the economy in order to retain skilled personnel and capital for the initial stages of their plans for reconstruction and industrialization. Article 26 of the Common Programme formulated in 1949 declared that 'the basic principle for economic construction of the People's Republic of China is to attain the goal of developing production . . . through the policy of taking into account both public and private interests and benefits to both labour and capital. . . .'

A distinction was made between the 'bureaucratic capitalists' and the 'national bourgeoisie'. The latter were described as an acceptable 'ally of the proletariat' whose existence was necessary during the transitional period of New Democracy. This national bourgeoisie were said to comprise 'the middle bourgeoisie'. Actually the term was apparently used, so far as business men were concerned, to describe those private manufacturers and traders who had remained in China, who had not been imprisoned or dispossessed of their property by the régime as 'counter-revolutionaries', and who were continuing, so far as lay within their power, to run their businesses. 'Bureaucratic capitalists' on the other hand seems simply to have meant those capitalists who had incurred the displeasure of the régime, in particular the comparatively few large-scale capitalists associated with the Nationalist régime such as the 'four families', Sung, Kung, Chen Li-fu, and Chen Li-kuo.

Once they were firmly entrenched, however, the Government

[1] Brandt, *Documentary History of Chinese Communism*, p. 303.

began to tighten their grip on private businesses. Early in 1950, as part of the measures adopted to ensure centralized control over the national economy, the new Government took the first steps in this direction. Private firms were called on to make full reports on current transactions, their financial status, and all aspects of their activities. On 31 December 1950 the 'Provisional Regulations for Private Enterprises' were promulgated, setting out in detail the conditions under which the private sector was to be allowed to operate. Businesses were required to submit their complete plans of production and sale for the approval of the Government (usually given through the appropriate ministry), and to distribute their earnings among dividends, welfare funds, and other uses in the proportions specified in the Regulations.

At the end of 1951 the Government introduced a major campaign against all owners of private firms. This was the 'Five Antis' movement directed against bribery, tax evasion, theft of state property, fraud, and theft of state economic secrets in business circles, paralleling the 'Three Antis' campaign (against corruption, bureaucracy, and waste) directed at the civil service. This campaign was waged with virulent intensity till half-way through the following year. Employees were encouraged to denounce their employers to the authorities if they were thought to indulge in any of the practices under attack. Mass meetings were held all over the country to whip up feeling against the capitalist class. The violence of the campaign seems to have been designed to cow completely the private business man and so to facilitate his subsequent absorption by the state. Massive fines were exacted from industrialists and merchants, and some businesses were confiscated outright. The Western press reported many suicides by Chinese business men.

The campaign was obviously primarily political in purpose. It aimed at discrediting private business in the eyes of the people and at driving the capitalist into subjection. It may also have been considered a convenient method of milking the capitalist class of their savings, urgently needed by the Government for their own capital construction programme.[1]

[1] Violent and highly publicized campaigns of this type have been a recurrent feature of life under the present régime and appear to represent an essential element in their technique of government. In addition to the 'Three Antis' and

In mid-1952 the campaign was soft-pedalled, perhaps because it was getting out of hand. It was laid down that officials should 'combine leniency with severity'. The Government undertook to help private businesses by loans, purchases, and new orders. This of course increased the dependence of business on the Government. In June 1952 a preparatory conference was held to establish the All-China Federation of Industry and Commerce which, while nominally representing the manufacturing classes, was to have the function of wielding a controlling influence on private enterprise and helping to integrate it where necessary into the state-planned economy.

This slight relaxation did not last for long. In October 1953 the Government called together a conference of private business men from all parts of the country—the National Congress of Industry and Commerce—at which it was made clear that the first aim of the Government was a fully socialist economy in which private industry would have no place, and that in the meanwhile the private sector was to be thoroughly integrated with the state-run economy. Li Wei-han, who is the Chinese leader responsible for all 'united front' activities—i.e. for all attempts to create a *modus vivendi* between non-Communist opinion and organizations and the Government—made quite clear to the business men the limitations within which they were to be allowed to operate.[1] He announced that the Government's policy towards private industry and commerce was to 'put it to good use, to keep it within proper bounds and to transform it'. The new 'general line' for the transitional stage before the accomplishment of socialism would mean 'the steady development of the socialist elements in the national economy,

the 'Five Antis' there have been a campaign against counter-revolutionaries, the 'Resist America, Aid Korea' campaign (the Korean War patriotic movement), the germ-warfare campaign (designed externally to discredit the Americans and internally to encourage higher standards of hygiene among the population), the 'Hu Feng' campaign (to suppress cultural heterodoxy), and the rectification campaign (to improve 'working style' among Communist and other officials), as well as the more immediately practical, and somewhat milder, campaigns, for example to popularize the marriage law, to encourage higher standards of literacy, and to 'increase production and practise economy'. Though each of these had some specific object in view, they seem to have been designed quite as much to keep the entire population on their toes, to maintain the revolutionary momentum, and to prevent any kind of relaxation which might encourage slackness or subversion.

[1] Report to National Congress of Industry and Commerce (BBC, Econ. Suppl. No. 88, 17 Nov. 1953).

the gradual reform of non-socialist elements and the gradual socialist industrialisation of the country . . .'. This would include the socialist transformation of private industry during the course of the transitional period, i.e. about three Five-Year Plans.

Enterprises beneficial to the national welfare would be used to the full, but many firms, it was claimed, were backward in their production and management, and would thus have to be 'reformed'. This apparently meant that such firms would at the very least be forced to adopt more modern methods, which in itself might involve being virtually taken over by the state. More often it was probably a euphemism to excuse the forcible absorption of small businesses into more economic units. In any case profit-seeking, described as the essential characteristic of the bourgeois, was inevitably harmful to the national welfare and must be restricted.

One of the most interesting passages of this statement, in the light of subsequent events, was that in which Li Wei-han described the advantages of state capitalism. This was clearly already planned as the transitional stage on the path towards nationalization for private businesses, just as the mutual-aid teams and the semi-socialist co-operative represented the transitional stage, before full-blooded collectivization, for the peasant. Under the state capitalist system private enterprise provides most of the capital assets and often managerial services, while overall direction, including sometimes the provision of further capital, is undertaken by the state. Profits are divided, part going to the state in taxation, part being ploughed back for future development and welfare facilities for the workers, and part being distributed in dividends. Owners are supposed to be guaranteed reasonable profits and given the opportunity to make use of their management and technical experience. The highest form of state capitalism was said to be the jointly operated state-private enterprise.

Although it was thus made quite clear to the private business man that he had not many more years to live, there was an element of ambiguity in the situation, as there was for the peasants at the same stage, in that neither could know how long the next stage was to last. Many business men may have been reassured by the apparently benevolent attitude adopted by Government spokesmen into thinking they had another dozen or so prosperous years ahead of them as owners of their concerns. In fact, no pronounced move was made by the Government during the next two years to hasten the take-over of private industry.

Throughout these years, however, and indeed from the very earliest days of the régime, there was a gradual process of absorption of the private sector by the state. For the most part this was not done by the outright nationalization either of industries or of individual firms, though in the early days some enterprises were taken over on the grounds that they had been owned by 'war criminals', 'collaborators', 'bureaucratic capitalists', by the Nationalist Government, or by former enemy governments. In most cases, however, the process took place by means of a process of gradual penetration. Thus, in the early days, when many firms may have wished to close down but were forbidden by law to lay off labour, the Government offered to guarantee the sale of an enterprise's output. Later the work of many factories was taken up with government orders and processing contracts. The extension of a government monopoly over virtually the whole field of the wholesale trade meant that most businesses were dependent on sales to government organizations. In addition all sources of credit were in the hands of the Government. In this way private enterprises rapidly became almost entirely dependent on the Government for their survival.

It is likely that in some cases the position became so difficult for private firms that they were only too glad to be taken over by the Government. This was the method adopted by the authorities in the case of most of the large foreign firms operating in China, for whom business was deliberately made impossible as a result of the control of wholesale contracts, raw-material supplies, and labour by the authorities. They were finally reduced to handing over their entire assets to the Government rather than continuing to pay wages, as they were by law obliged to do, to employees kept idle as a result of the Government's policies. In consequence the Government obtained assets worth hundreds of millions of pounds (the

British property alone was valued at £200 million), without paying compensation.

Partly as a result of these methods the proportion of the total value of industrial production represented by private industry decreased from 39 per cent. in 1952 to 16 per cent. in 1955 (though these figures, of course, primarily reflect the growth of the state industries rather than the decline of the private sector). By the end of 1955 about 82 per cent. of the total output of private industry was devoted to goods processed for, ordered or purchased by, the state. At the same time the proportion of total output supplied by the joint state-private enterprises recommended by Li Wei-han had grown to 16 per cent.

The process of assimilation of private enterprise, both industrial and commercial, by the state developed rapidly towards the end of 1955 and in the early part of 1956. This movement represented the counterpart in private industry of the growth of co-operatives occurring at about the same time in the agricultural sector. A speed-up of the 'socialization' of private industry and commerce had been foreshadowed during the second half of 1955. On 31 December 1955 a *People's Daily* editorial, having drawn attention to the big growth in co-operation in the countryside then taking place, demanded that the 'socialist transformation of capitalist industry' should also be intensified by the introduction of joint state-private operation of an entire trade, both in industry and commerce, and by the adoption of a fixed rate of interest for the distribution of profits to private industrialists or business men engaged in joint operation. About the same time reports began to appear that in various large cities one trade after another had applied for joint state-private operation. A wave of agitation and publicity similar to that which took place in the agricultural field was launched all over the country.

The campaign was brief and very intense. Within a few months most of the private firms throughout the country had been absorbed in joint state-private enterprises. A change was also effected in the method of distributing profits in state-private enterprises. This had formerly been done each year by dividing an agreed figure for profits into four shares and apportioning one-fourth to the owner; this was nominally arrived at by a process of negotiation between the owner and representatives of the state, though, since the owner had no legal sanctions to apply, it is unlikely that his views counted for much. Under the new system a fixed rate of interest was paid. The interest was paid on the capital value of the business as assessed by the owner and agreed by the responsible government agency—generally the local branch of the Ministry of Internal Commerce. Under the revised system the business man probably again had no option but to submit to arbitrary valuations of his business by the local authority.

Normally the former owners were given jobs in the new state-private enterprise, in order to take advantage of their managerial skill and experience. In such cases, in addition to receiving dividends, they were to be paid salaries on the same scale as the managers of state-operated enterprises.

The absorption of the private firms was accompanied by a process of 'rationalization'. All the privately owned flour mills in Peking, for example, were brought together under a single general management so as to secure the co-ordination of their production plans and the pooling of their capital funds. Fifteen plants engaged in the manufacture of electrical appliances were merged into six factories, each specializing in transformers, switches, meters, insulating materials, or ventilators. This pattern was repeated all over the country. In Shanghai, where in 1955 there were over 26,000 private firms engaged in industry, employing some 400,000 workers, it was planned to transform 80 per cent.—on the basis of production value—of these firms into joint state-private concerns, with the state as the 'senior partner', in 1956 and 90 per cent. in 1957. But as time went on the tempo increased. In his report to the Congress of the CCP on 16 September 1956 Chou En-lai reported that by the end of June that year 99 per cent. of capitalist enterprises in terms of output value had come under joint state-private operation.

It is clear that a good deal of disruption accompanied this transformation. In some cases local officials seem to have carried out violent overhauls of the whole organization of the firms engaged in a particular trade, without regard to the disturbance caused to production and existing trading arrangements. It was reported that in some places the merger of factories was 'blindly carried out to excess, with the result that the original supply and marketing procedure or co-operative relationships were dislocated, leading to less variety and products of poorer quality, overcrowding of workshops with equipment, and difficulty in making arrangements for stable living conditions for workers'. Thus in February 1956 the State Council had to issue a directive that private enterprises should normally, for about six months from the approval of joint ownership, carry on their operations as previously, before any reorganization took place.[1]

Although official accounts have depicted the former private owners of these firms as entering whole-heartedly and even 'joyfully' into the new joint enterprises, Chen Shu-tung, President of the National Federation of Private Industry and Commerce, in an address to a special session of the Federation's Executive Committee, admitted that there were some business men who 'had no sympathy with socialist transformation' and who 'maintained an attitude of passive resistance'. He called for a special effort to root out 'counter-revolutionaries' and, in appealing for co-operation with the Government, said that they would have to rely especially on the younger 'progressives'.[2] These and other similar statements are an indication of the resistance of many private owners whose factories and firms were then 'entering socialism' to the developments that were taking place.

On occasion the business men even expressed their dissatisfaction in public, and in remarkably outspoken terms. At a meeting of the Democratic Construction Association, a private business man's organization, held in Peking in July 1956, one delegate 'pointed out certain unjust relations between the state and private sides in some enterprises and poor working methods by some Government representatives in such enterprises'. Another criticized the Association for 'inadequately raising the demands of the industrialists and business men'. Another said that 'mutual supervision' (i.e. by the CP and other political parties of each other) 'would help the Communist Party to overcome its defects and improve its leadership'.[3]

During the summer of 1956 the Government went a stage

---

[1] State Council Decisions on Transformation of Private Enterprises, 10 Feb. 1956 (*NCNA*, 14 Feb. 1956).
[2] *NCNA*, 20 Nov. 1955.   [3] Ibid., 12 July 1956.

farther. They began to undertake the incorporation of small traders, pedlars, and handicraftsmen into co-operatives. This was to be done 'voluntarily' but the Government would 'be prepared to assist in organizing them into such co-operative groups to help them to solve their livelihood difficulties and the problem of their business arrangement'. By September 1956 90 per cent. of individual handicraftsmen were incorporated in industrial producers' co-operatives, producers' groups, or supply and marketing co-operatives. State shops would serve as wholesalers for the co-operative groups of small traders and pedlars. They would supply commodities and raise loans from the banks on behalf of the co-operative group. It was almost certainly intended that by these means small shops and traders would become completely dependent on the parent state shop and finally be absorbed in it. Pedlars too would probably finally become agents of larger trading organizations or be abolished altogether. The handicrafts co-operatives, however, were perhaps intended to be permanent; there have been a good many of these since the start of the régime, and there could have been no possible advantage in incorporating handicraftsmen in larger and more closely knit organizations, at least so long as their products remained competitive with machine-made goods.

There were no reports of active opposition or serious unrest either among business men or shopkeepers in face of these sweeping changes. The speed and relentlessness of the campaign, and the powerlessness of the capitalists as a class, probably made it clear to them that they had no alternative to accepting their new status. They could only try to get the most favourable terms possible in the process. Many owners had no doubt been expecting the blow for some time before it fell. They were certainly well aware of the relentlessness of the Government in pursuit of their declared aims and thus perhaps recognized, with characteristic Chinese resignation, the hopelessness of resistance.

Private business men were left in no doubt that even what little independence remained to them was not to last long. In a speech at the People's Congress in June 1956 Chen Yun suggested that the dividends of from 1 to 6 per cent., payable to the former owners of state-private enterprises according to the profits earned, should be universally altered to a fixed interest of 5 per cent. irrespective of the losses or gains of the enterprises, though in a few cases this amount might be exceeded. A directive of the State Administrative Council of 30 July laid down that this proposal should be generally adopted. Later that year, however, there were clear hints that the payments of interest to former owners of businesses would not be continued much longer. Finally, in December, in a speech to the All-China Federation of Industry and Commerce, Po I-po stated that such payments would only be assured for a further seven years, i.e. until the end of the second Five-Year Plan in 1962, when it was hoped that the period of 'socialist transformation' would be finally completed; only in a few cases, if business men were in economic difficulties, would payments be continued after that time. Some business men were said to have given up their interest payments voluntarily, anxious to renounce their status as capitalists and join the ranks of the proletariat.

As a result of these operations private businesses, even the smallest, had by the end of 1956 been virtually absorbed into the state-run economy. The owners themselves seem to have been effectively cowed into submission. At the end of the National Congress of the All-China Federation of Industry and Commerce in December 1956, the assembled industrialists and business men obligingly passed a resolution[1] declaring that they would 'strengthen our self-transformation, and unequivocally acknowledge the consistency between the State and our own interests'; they would 'devote our technical training and experience, which are useful to production and business management, to the cause of the socialist construction of our fatherland, and be diligent, honest, faithful, responsible and enthusiastic in socialist emulation drives . . .'; and they would accept the leadership of the state element in their enterprises and 'strengthen the unity between the State and private sectors of our enterprises by means of criticism and self-criticism under the leadership of the CCP and the People's Government'.

Despite the abject spirit expressed in this resolution, in practice there were evidently fairly frequent clashes between

[1] BBC, Econ. Suppl. No. 248, 10 Jan. 1957.

the state representatives in the new 'joint-owned' enterprises
and the representatives of the private side, who in many cases
were now acting as managers. At the Congress of the All-China
Federation of Industry and Commerce it was admitted that in
some cases 'these relations had not been at all smooth'. Some
former private business men were accused of being unco-opera-
tive and showing remnants of their former bourgeois mentality.
But there were also many criticisms in the other direction.
These were particularly outspoken at the time of the rectification and 'hundred flowers' movement during the spring of 1957.
Much publicity was given to complaints by the private side of
industry of rudeness from the trade union and state representatives and of inefficiency by the state-appointed administrators
who now controlled them. The business men claimed that the
state side adopted a dictatorial tone, and did not allow them
any share in policy or personnel decisions, so that their experience and technical qualifications were being wasted. Some even
demanded an inquiry into the injustices committed during the
'Five-Antis' movement six years before.[1]

It is evident that the Government themselves were by this
time beginning to realize that there were dangers in carrying
out the process of 'socialist transformation' in such a way that
the skills developed by the private business men in their long
experience of trading activity were lost, and the forms of
organization which had been built up to serve the existing
needs of the market were indiscriminately broken down. In his
speech to the CCP Congress in September 1956 Chen Yun
stressed the fact that 'an overwhelming majority of our national
capitalists are endowed with knowledge of modern production
techniques', which the country urgently needed. 'The national
bourgeoisie, including the intellectuals of this class, still consti-
tutes a class of the higher bracket', and to make use of their
skills would be in the interest of the Chinese working class as
a whole.[2]

Thus the 'measures adopted by the economic organs of the

[1] Non-Party members of the state organizations made similar complaints. Some
complained of discrimination because they were members of one of the minority
parties or former capitalists. One engineer said that 'cadres did not care whether
people were efficient or not. All they cared about was whether people were Party
members.'
[2] NCNA, 21 Sept. 1956.

State for restricting capitalist industry and commerce have become unnecessary'. The system of guaranteeing, and so controlling, the production of factories by government contracts would in many cases be abandoned, and they would in future produce only for the market. State retail shops at the basic level, as well as the wholesale agencies, would be enabled to purchase direct from factories. Small business men and pedlars should be enabled to run their own businesses within a co-operative team. The monopoly of import trade by the state agencies would be broken up: former private firms, now run as joint state-private enterprises, would be asked to set up import stores to engage in business formerly handled by them, and of which they had unique experience. 'Regulations on market control which were designed to restrict the speculative activities of capitalist industry and commerce' must be abolished and private merchants given greater scope in the marketing of subsidiary agricultural produce.[1] Thus, after less than a year of the socialist transformation in industry, the free market, and even to some extent the profit motive, were allowed to put in a subdued appearance once more.

By the beginning of 1957 a good many of the former owners of the private enterprises were coming to wish they could throw off their status as former capitalists, even if this meant abandoning the interest payments on their former businesses which, in the case of a small business or shop, might be quite small. By continuing to receive the interest, and remaining under the official designation of capitalist, they suffered various disadvantages. They were excluded from the trades unions and thus from insurance and pension benefits. They suffered social discredit, especially in the eyes of the official world, through whose favour alone they could now hope to advance themselves. Many business men at public meetings stressed their desire to be considered as members of the working class. One suggested that the seven years' interest on their former assets should be converted into state bonds redeemable over twenty years. But, although a few social security benefits have been granted to those capitalists having a low income from their dividends, for the most part these demands have been rejected.

[1] See below, pp. 185–6.

Only in a few of the big towns have private business men been completely abolished. In Tientsin it was suddenly announced in 1958 that all the 37,000 remaining business men had been 'reformed' during a single week's campaign. In Peking a thousand capitalists were said to have asked to join in the campaign for personal labour by working at the benches of their own factories, so that they could shed their bourgeois mentality and become absorbed into the proletariat. Many all over the country had asked to hand over their real estate in order to receive interest payments from the state in place of rent. In some places, including Peking, all privately owned rented property was in fact taken over by the state in July 1958.

The Government were from the start committed by their ideology to the elimination of all privately owned forms of economic organization in China. Although, at any rate in the case of retail trade, no very useful economic purpose can have been achieved by the process, their aim has now been virtually fulfilled. The transformation of private businesses, like the similar change in the field of agriculture, was apparently brought about, not mainly by physical coercion or outright expropriation, but by the application of the strongest possible political pressure short of compulsion, coupled with almost unchallengeable financial inducements and penalties. By these means the authorities have been able to bring about virtually the same results as by wholesale nationalization, with only the payment of a few years' dividends by way of compensation. Now that ideological requirements have been satisfied, it seems that some relaxation may take place, and that the Government may be prepared to sanction, if not any return to private ownership, at least some decentralization and an increase in independence for the individual economic unit.[1]

[1] See above, p. 61.

IX

THE NEW ECONOMIC GEOGRAPHY AND THE DEVELOPMENT OF COMMUNICATIONS

ALTHOUGH the first Five-Year Plan envisaged a nation-wide scheme of industrialization, the scale of development has in fact been far from uniform over the whole country. The main weight of industrialization during that Plan was concentrated in the northern part of the country. There are understandable reasons for this.

In the first place nearly all the major deposits of coal and iron lie in the north: the most important deposits of coal are in Shansi, while the biggest supplies of iron ore are in the North East and in Chahar. Secondly, apart from some development of light industry in Shanghai and in some other coastal and Yangtze ports, industrial development before the present régime came to power was almost entirely concentrated in the north. This was partly because of the presence of iron and coal resources in Manchuria, but even more because the industries in that area had received large-scale development under the Japanese, who, deficient themselves in both coal and iron, had made the region one of the chief workshops for their drive against East Asia. As a result, almost all of the plant for the development of heavy industry in China was concentrated in the North East. Thirdly, the railway system was, mainly through Japanese and Russian construction, far better developed in the North East and in North China (though not in the North West) than in other parts of the country. Fourthly, for strategic reasons it may have been considered wise for the first main centres of industry to be situated in parts of the country some way inland, and as close as possible to the protective mass of the Soviet Union.

Within the northern part of the country as a whole there are three main regions: Manchuria, North China (in China Proper), and the North West. In the early stages of the Plan, while new plants for other regions were being planned and designed, development was concentrated in the North East (Manchuria). In 1952 Manchuria probably already accounted for about 50 per cent. of coal output, about 80 per cent. of power capacity, and about 90 per cent. of the iron and steel output of the country. Vigorous expansion took place in Anshan, the nation's industrial show-piece (iron and steel), Harbin (heavy industry), Fushin (coal), Fushun (coal and steel), Dairen (iron and steel), and Penchi (iron ore, steel, and coal). Most of these centres had been intensively developed during the Japanese occupation, stripped by the Soviet Union, and in due course re-equipped with Soviet aid. Plants for the manufacture of machine tools have been set up in Mukden, Tsitsihar, and Changchun. A big new plant to manufacture chemical fertilizer has been built with Soviet aid at Kirin, which is to become the principal centre of the country's chemical industry. And in the very far north the largest heavy machinery plant in the country has been built at Fulaerchi, where a completely new industrial city has been set up.

There has also been considerable development in North China. This possesses rich deposits of coal and a certain amount of iron. Thus the Taiyuan and Shihchingshan iron and steel centres have been developed—Taiyuan is so far the only centre of heavy industry to be expanded on a scale comparable with the North East, having, besides the iron and steel works, heavy machine plants and factories for electrical and aeronautical equipment. But work has now started on the creation of a huge iron and steel centre with a planned output of 1·5 million tons of steel at Paotow. There has at the same time been some development in and around Peking, where a new industrial complex, started under the Japanese, has been expanded and developed. And in the last year or two there has been a big expansion in Tientsin.

The development of the North West, i.e. Sinkiang, Kansu, Shensi, and Chinghai has been primarily in mining. A good deal of mining development in Sinkiang had been undertaken by the Soviet Union when the province was virtually under her control. This was continued by the joint Sino-Soviet mixed companies, which were set up when the present Chinese Government came to power. After these companies had been returned to Chinese control, the Chinese continued a policy of vigorous development in the North West. Industrial expansion has been particularly vigorous at Sian and Lanchow, on the railway being built to the western border.

When the régime first came to power, substantial Chinese forces were sent to Sinkiang to establish and to maintain Chinese control of the area, which for many years had been at best precarious—the Soviet Union had in recent years exploited the weakness of Chinese authority and the difficulty of communication with China Proper to acquire a wide measure of control for themselves. These Chinese forces have remained in the province until the present time, and the Chinese authorities have made use of them to supplement the very exiguous local population in developing agriculture and exploiting what natural resources have so far been discovered. Newly discovered oil deposits are being developed at Karamai in the far north of the province, and the existing oil installations at Yumen in Kansu have been considerably expanded. A considerable part of Chinese activity so far, however, has consisted in exploring the resources of the area. There are said to be deposits of copper, lead, zinc, and other non-ferrous metals, as well as a considerable amount of oil, within the province.

Outside these three areas development during the first Plan was on a more restricted scale. Light industries have been set up almost throughout China. New textile mills have been built in the cotton-growing areas of Hopei, Shensi, and Honan, instead of on the east coast as before. One of the features of development policy at first was the comparative decline in the importance of Shanghai, perhaps regarded as a symbol of the semi-colonial past. Before the war, with Manchuria under Japanese control, Shanghai accounted for about half of total Chinese industrial output. Most of the rest had been concentrated in the three coastal ports of Tientsin, Tsingtao, and Canton, and the Yangtze port of Hankow. The present régime appears to have had the aim of distributing the industrial capacity of the country more widely, and none of these cities was at first scheduled for any very large-scale industrial development. In the early days of the régime the authorities spoke indeed of a very considerable reduction in the population of Shanghai. These plans have now been modified. Recent declarations have stressed that, while the development of the interior is to continue, the importance of the coastal provinces must not be neglected. It is fairly clear that, as a result of discrimination by the central authorities, the industrial capacity of Shanghai and other cities was being seriously under-exploited.

So far, therefore, none of the cities of the south have been developed on the scale of the new industrial centres of the north. There has thus over the last few years been a considerable shift of the areas of industrial development in the country away from the east coast and towards the north. The primary reason for the high degree of industrialization of the east-coast and Yangtze ports before was that these represented the points of access to China for the West, and thus were the places where the Westerners naturally sought permission to settle for trading purposes and, at a later stage, to set up industries. They were also nearest the sources of imported raw materials and more favourably placed to export finished products (though few of the Chinese industries were large exporters). Today these conditions no longer apply; most raw materials come from within China, and many are situated in the north and west; and imported equipment comes primarily overland from the Soviet Union. The pattern of Chinese economic geography has thus been radically altered.

In their plans for the future, however, the Chinese Government have shown that they intend to pay greater attention to the development of the south. Indeed their members quite often speak of the need for a well-balanced development in which all parts of the country shall share. Work has started on a huge new iron and steel works, on a similar scale to that being built at Paotow, at Hankow. Substantial iron and steel works are also being built at Tayeh in Hupeh, at Liuchow in Kwangsi, at Antung, at Kunming, at Shanghai, and at Canton. Chengtu is to become an important centre for the machine-tool industry. There is to be development of non-ferrous metals in Chungking, where there is already a growing steel industry. And the skilled labour of Shanghai is now to be used to make it a centre for the chemical, radio, machine-building, and shipping industries.

As a result of this distribution of industry new trading patterns are emerging. Nearly all movements of steel, heavy machinery, and most other industrial equipment are at present from the North East to other parts of the country. A certain amount of coal, iron, and steel is also sent from North China, especially from Shansi. From the south-west there are exports of non-ferrous metals which are imported mainly into North and East China. The main movements of grain are from the surplus areas of the North East (dry grains) and the Yangtze basin (rice). Raw cotton is exported from the producing areas in North China and the Central South to the mills on the east coast. Light engineering products and consumer goods are sent from Shanghai, Tientsin, and other east-coast towns, which are importing areas for agricultural products. In general the North East and the east coast are the prosperous parts of China, having comparatively highly developed industry as well as adequate agricultural resources, while the south-west and the far south, which, except for Szechwan, have no large agricultural surplus and little industrial development, may prove to be the backward areas of the country.

In order to secure the widest interchange of the products of industry and agriculture, there has been a vigorous drive by the Government to stimulate the growth of internal trade between the different regions of China. In this way they hope to enlarge the effective market within the country, to bring about the most efficient division of labour and resources, and, above all, to eliminate shortages. In countries which are attempting to achieve very rapid industrialization there is an urgent need to ensure that the scanty available supplies of consumer goods are as widely distributed as possible. This is necessary, on the one hand, in order to eliminate all local shortages which might bring about inflationary pressure, and on the other in order to give workers and peasants some incentive to increase their earning power and thus to bring about increases in production. The need for expanding trade in the countryside is particularly important if it is hoped to persuade the peasants to make large supplies of their produce available in the form of deliveries and sales to the local marketing organization: unless there are supplies of goods on which they may consider it worth-while to spend the money they acquire from such sales, they may prefer to hold their wealth in kind and to withhold their produce from the marketing organizations. By securing the maximum interflow of goods between town and country, the Chinese Government have hoped to avoid the disastrous consequences (political as well as economic) of the 'scissors' effect—the imbalance between the peasants' purchasing power and the available supply of consumer goods—which occurred in the Soviet Union during the 1920's.

The establishment of the state trading companies in the early days of the régime has given the Government their principal tool for achieving this aim. In time the control of domestic trade fell almost exclusively into government hands. The share of wholesale trade handled by state and co-operative commerce rose from about 59 per cent. in 1953 to about 90 per cent. in 1954, and 96 per cent. in 1955. With this machinery under their control the Government have set as one of their aims a big increase in total retail sales. One of the targets of the Five-Year Plan, parallel with the targets for increased production, was an increase in the total volume of these sales. It was hoped that they would reach a figure of 48·9 billion yuan in 1957, or 80 per cent. more than in 1952.

The Government have devoted particular attention to the problem of stimulating trade between the towns and the surrounding countryside. This involved on the one hand persuading local manufacturers and artisans that it was worth their while to send their produce to market in the country, and on the other encouraging new habits in consumer spending on the part of the peasants. They developed a regular campaign, calling meetings throughout the country to encourage trading contacts on these lines. Special government motor-transport companies were set up to assist in the development of new trading contacts between town and country.

The development of new regions and the stimulation of commercial exchanges between them has demanded a very considerable expansion of communications. During the first few years of the new régime there was intensive development of the railway system. There were several reasons for this. Military and political control of the enormous area of the

Chinese mainland depends on an efficient and comprehensive system of communications. The Government's efforts to counteract inflation required the rapid movement of goods to prevent shortages. The long-term aim of industrialization demanded effective transportation from one area of the country to another. During the first two years of the Government's existence something like one-fifth of the total amount spent by the Government on economic reconstruction was devoted to the rehabilitation of the railways, and there were further big increases on the amounts spent on this in 1951 and 1952. A large part of these sums was spent not on the construction of new lines but on the rehabilitation of old ones. Even today, although 4,000–5,000 miles of new track have probably been built since the régime came to power, the total length (about 20,000 miles) shows no very startling increase on the pre-war total (a few pre-war lines have been allowed to go out of use). And the railway system is still quite inadequate to cope with the heavy volume of traffic, which the concentration of industry in a few key centres has intensified.

In Manchuria there already existed at the time when the new Government came to power a well-developed system of communications, including about half the total length of railway in the country. This network centred round the two principal lines, the west–east line serving Vladivostok, developed by the Russians, formerly the Chinese Eastern Railway, and the north–south line, serving the Liaotung Peninsula, developed by the Japanese, formerly the South Manchuria Railway. Thus no new construction was necessary to serve the great industrial complex being developed in Manchuria, though there was some replacement to overcome the anomalies caused by differing gauges.

In both the north and the North West, however, there has been considerable new development. In the north a line has been built from Chining in Suiyuan to Erhlien on the Outer Mongolian border, linking up with a railway coming down from Ulan Bator, the capital of Outer Mongolia, which is in turn linked with the Trans-Siberian railway. This line has considerably shortened the route for transporting materials from Russia to North China. In the North West an even more

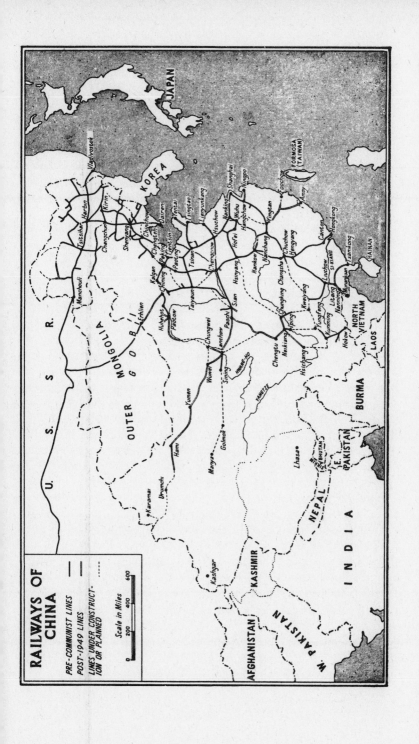

RAILWAYS OF CHINA

PRE-COMMUNIST LINES
POST-1949 LINES
LINES UNDER CONSTRUCT-
ION OR PLANNED

Scale in Miles

0   200   400   600

ambitious project has been started. This is the construction of
a line running from Tienshui (which is itself linked with lines
running to Peking in the north-east and Canton in the south)
through Lanchow and Yumen, the oil centre, across the Gobi
Desert and the whole length of Sinkiang to the western border of
the province, where it will join up with the Soviet railway system.
This route will then probably become the main link between
the Soviet Union and China. It will in any case immensely
improve Chinese communications with Sinkiang, which until
fairly recently was a three-month journey from Peking.

Another line has been completed between Chungking and
Chengtu, and extended to Paochi, on the east–west line now
being extended to Sinkiang, so linking the south-west with the
North West.[1] Another extension is to be built from Chengtu
in the other direction, and will reach to Kunming in the far
south-western corner of China, thus forming a second main
north–south rail axis running parallel to that going down from
Peking through Hankow to Canton.

The fourth main new railway project, now completed, has
been the building of a line from Liuchow in Kwangsi to
Munankuan on the Indo-China border, from which there is an
extension to Hanoi and the seaport Haiphong in North Vietnam, which the Chinese are beginning to develop as an important port of access to China. There is a similar line from
Kunming to the Indo-Chinese border. In addition an important
new line from Yingtan to Amoy, for the first time effectively
opening up Fukien to the interior, has been built. There are
plans for new railways linking Hankow and Sian along the Han
valley, and from Sian to Chungwei in Kansu, from Sining in
Chinghai to Manya in the far west of the same province, from
Kweiyang in Kweichow east to Chuchow, so linking with the
north–south line to Canton, from Lanchow to the new centre
at Paotow, from the Golmok oilfields in Chinghai to Lhasa,
and from Chengtu to Hsichang on the Tibetan border.

[1] The construction of this line gave an example of the failings which are liable
to occur as a result of the intensive pressure for quick results under which Chinese
engineers work, as well as of their lack of experience in many fields. The line was
originally said to have been completed half-way through 1956. Tests by the railway
authorities, however, revealed that there were nearly 200 places on the line which
were considered unsafe and would have to be reconstructed. The line was not
finally completed until the end of 1957, nearly a year and a half later.

A severe limitation of the present railway system in China is the fact that many of the more important lines are still single-track lines along a great part of their length. As a result the Government are at present devoting considerable efforts to double-tracking the principal lines. A further important development which will immensely improve rail communications in China is the recent construction of the 1,700-metre road and rail bridge across the Yangtze at Hankow. This for the first time allows through traffic from the north to Canton —until now trains and motor vehicles have had to be ferried across the Yangtze. A double-track rail bridge has also been constructed at Chungking.

Since China has at present very few lorries, the development of roads has played a far less important part in the programme of communications construction: where railways do not exist, water transport is still in most parts, as it has been for many centuries, the most important medium of communication. Nevertheless a certain amount of work has been done in the construction of highways and in the repair of old ones.

The most important new highways built have been those to link Sian and Lanchow in the North West with Peking, and the network of routes which have been built to Tibet. One of the roads in Tibet leads north-west into Sinkiang and right across to the western border of the province, where it will be linked with the Soviet highway system; another goes to the north-east to Chinghai in North West China; while a third has been built along the traditional route into Tibet from Szechwan. Further highways are planned to link Kunming and Hokow on the North Vietnam border, and to join Chinghai and Sinkiang. There were said to be 250,000 km. of highway in use at the end of 1957.

By far the greater part of Chinese road transport at the moment, for example for the transport of building materials and for local trade, is by such primitive means as donkeys, mules, camels, and even hand-carts. In the second half of 1956 the production of the Chinese-built 'liberation' lorries at the factory at Changchun started. Production is said now to be running at the rate of nearly 20,000 a year. The total number of lorries in use in China is nevertheless still minute in relation to the size of the country. And apart from questions of production, the use of motor transport in China may be inhibited by shortage of petrol. It is perhaps for these reasons that Po I-po, speaking to the National People's Congress in 1957, called for the further development of the traditional methods of transport such as animal-drawn carts, hand-carts, and wooden boats.

Possibly for the same reason, or because of shortage of aircraft, air transport does not seem to have played a large part so far in the development of communications in China. It has been developed principally in the northern provinces, Sinkiang, Kansu, Inner Mongolia, and the North East, formerly served by the Sino-Soviet companies, and in some remote parts such as Yunnan. The total route mileage was said to be about 20,000 miles by the end of 1957. Considerable efforts have been expended on the construction of a lavish airport at Peking, which is claimed to be the largest and most modern in the Far East. Chinese airlines are now using the Chinese-constructed AN-2, and during 1958 there has been a considerable development of local provincial airlines, run by the provincial authorities and using their planes principally to link provincial capitals with more remote parts of each province.

Big increases in the use of water transport have been claimed by the authorities. This applies both to the coastal traffic which, being more economical for long distances than the railways, is of great importance in China, and to the traffic along the rivers and canals, in particular along the Yangtze which has for thousands of years been the principal means of communication to Hankow, Ichang, and Chungking. The Chinese transportation companies have probably had to rely to a large extent on junks and other small craft, mainly drawn by tugs or mechanically propelled, for these purposes, and from the accounts given it appears that the available craft are now used highly intensively. The Chinese are now, however, constructing small ships of their own and claim to have successfully launched freighters of 5,000 tons and over.[1]

---

[1] According to the Ministry of Communications, China possessed at the end of 1956 twice as much inland and coastal shipping tonnage as in 1949. During 1956 cargo ships and tug-drawn barges on inland waterways moved 4·7 times more ton-km. of freight than in 1952. By the end of 1958, 144,000 km. of waterways were in use.

Parallel with this development of rivers and canals as means of communication has gone a huge effort to control the waters of those rivers liable to flood. Owing to the flatness of the land over most of North China down as far as the Yangtze, and to the relatively short periods of intensely heavy rain in the summer, a large proportion of the rivers in that part of the country are subject to flooding, and when they do, spread over a very large area of the country, causing great damage. On an average there is said to have been, over the centuries, a serious flood disaster every two or three years; in some years hundreds of thousands might be drowned in such floods and some 20–30 million left homeless. The rivers which have been principally responsible for these disasters have been the Yellow River (China's sorrow), the Yangtze, and the Huai. The Yellow River has on occasions completely changed its course and debouched, into the sea some hundreds of miles away from its previous mouth.

These enormous river-control projects are carried out by huge teams of labour, consisting in part of groups considered as criminal, 'anti-revolutionaries', and others out of favour with the régime, working under the principle of 'reform through labour', but mainly of teams of peasants drawn from the locality of the particular project, or from the areas likely to benefit from it, more or less conscripted to contribute their labour.[1] The most important of the works carried out so far has been the Huai River conservation scheme: there was a particularly serious inundation of the Huai in 1949, and it was perhaps for this reason that the Chinese Government gave priority to it. According to Chinese official sources, something like 20 million people were engaged in the work at one time or another, though there never seem to have been more than about 2·5 million working on it at any one time, and some of these may have been only working part-time. As a result of these labours huge embankments have been created, and large reservoirs are being constructed on the upper reaches of the river for the storage of flood water, which is subsequently used for irrigation purposes. The authorities claim very big increases

[1] Some road construction is also carried out by 'voluntary labour of peasants and handicraftsmen'.

(50 per cent.) in output from the irrigated areas as a result of the project. The work has not, however, been entirely effective in its main purpose, since although the area drained by the Huai River largely escaped the effects of the serious floods which occurred elsewhere in 1954, flooding occurred there both in 1956 and 1957. The authorities have since claimed, however, that their plans have not yet been completed, and that new work should succeed in overcoming the danger of flood by 1962. Other important water-control projects have been the reservoirs constructed on the Yung-ting River in Hopei, and on the Ching River, a section of the Yangtze. Work has begun on a big hydro-electric power station, which will be able to generate 580,000 kw. of electricity on the Hsinan River, south-west of Shanghai. Along the Yellow River a series of multi-purpose schemes are being put in hand, which will provide irrigation, generate power, and improve navigation. The most important of them is that at Sanmen on the middle reaches of the river. This is to provide irrigation for an area equal to one-third of all the arable land in England, and to produce 1·1 million kw. of electric power. It is claimed that the storage capacity of the dam will exceed that of the Boulder and Grand Coulee dams combined. An important factor in the success of the project will be the anti-erosion work to be done on the plateau of Shensi, Kansu, and Shansi to prevent loose soil blowing, or being washed, into the river and silting it up.

There are even more ambitious projects for the future. Provisional plans for the development of the Yangtze have provided for a series of huge dams, including one near Paotung on the Szechwan–Hupeh border, which is to be 400 ft. high and generate 15 million kw. of electricity. A plan for the development of the Heilungkiang (Amur) River on the Russian border has been drawn up in conjunction with the Soviet Union, including the construction of five dams to generate 1 million kw. each, and of canals linking the river to the river system of South Manchuria, so creating a new industrial region in the area. There is a preliminary plan for the Sungari, and one for the Sikiang (West River) is in preparation. Halfway through 1959 China announced an ambitious ten-year plan for the further development of inland waterways. This included a continuous line of canals and rivers stretching from the Amur in the north, by way of a restored and enlarged Grand Canal, to the Yangtze and thence to Canton. There will also be a number of lateral branches to the ports of the east coast.

The Chinese Government's efforts to bring about a wider distribution of industry, to secure the fullest possible exchanges of goods between different areas, and to develop communications have all been conditioned in part by political considerations. One of the principal reasons why previous régimes in China lost control of the country was that individual areas, self-sufficient in resources and almost entirely cut off as a result of poor communications, have, under the authority of powerful local officials or war-lords, become more and more remote from the authority of the central Government, until finally they have become virtually independent units. The Communist Government have been anxious from the start to restore and to maintain the unity of the country. It was partly in order to obviate the fissiparous tendencies which had endangered previous régimes that they have made such efforts to ensure that every part of the country should be firmly linked with all others and thus merged into an organic political entity. But in the process they have also begun to weld China, as never before, into a single, integrated economic unit.

X

THE ORGANIZATION OF LABOUR

TRADE unions in China today are described by the authorities as 'mass organizations of all manual and non-manual workers living entirely or mainly on their wages'. They are thus composed almost exclusively of the industrial proletariat. They do not include the peasants, shopkeepers, or craftsmen, although clerical staff and certain types of managerial personnel are members. The 'supreme leading body of the trade unions' is the All-China Federation of Trade Unions. The total membership of the Communist-controlled trade unions increased from 800,000 in 1945 to 12·45 million in 1955. In 1958 total membership was said to be 16 million.

In Communist countries the words 'trade union' are used to describe an entirely different type of organization from that which we know under the name. According to Lenin and all subsequent Marxist writers, trade unions represent one form of 'transmission belt' for making contact between the Communist Party and the rest of the population. Thus, although the Chinese trade unions are instructed in their constitution 'to show constant concern over the improvement of the material and cultural life and the working conditions of the entire body of workers, technical personnel, and staff members', they are primarily designed as a public relations body, and a means of organizing and controlling industrial workers. Their principal officers are Communist Party members, whose loyalty to the Party overrides that to the interests of the members of the union. They have no part to play in negotiating wage rates, which are simply laid down by the authorities and are not subject to discussion. Strikes (known as 'sabotage') are not, of course, permitted in Communist countries.

Membership of trade unions, according to the Trade Unions Constitution of 1953, is 'voluntary'. In practice various pressures have had the effect of drawing practically all industrial workers into the system. Some social-security benefits are only available to trade unionists. In addition it is almost certain that strong pressure is brought to bear, by officials, Communist Party members, and other union members, on the individual worker to join.

Various regulations and other documents give some idea of the role which is intended by the authorities for the trade unions within the society they are building. In July and August 1949 three sets of provisional regulations governing relations between employers and workers were adopted by a National Conference on Trade Union Work convened at that time. These were concerned with relations between workers and employers in private undertakings; the drawing up of collective agreements in private undertakings; and the procedure for the settlement of labour disputes. They were intended as 'model regulations', and in a directive of 22 November 1949 to its member unions, the All-China Federation of Trade Unions instructed the higher trade union bodies in different regions and cities to arrange for their adoption by the local authorities. As a result, early in 1950 local regulations, based on the model circulated, were introduced and enforced in Peking, Shanghai, Tientsin, Hankow, Canton, and other commercial and industrial centres. Early in the same year the regulations were approved and published by the Standing Committee of the All-China Federation of Trade Unions. These rules were incorporated with some revision into later legislation, and represent the basic provisions on industrial relations in the field of private enterprise. Their counterpart for the state industries was 'The Outline of Labour Regulations for State-Operated Enterprises' issued in 1954.[1]

The main provisions dealt with freedom of association, collective agreements, engagement and dismissal, wages, hours of work, labour discipline and welfare, the status of apprentices, and labour disputes. Questions not catered for in the regulations were intended to be covered by separate collective agreements or individual contracts of employment for each concern.

'In principle', hours of work in industry were fixed at eight to ten a day. Working hours could be reduced or increased 'by agreement' between workers and the employer, but the daily

[1] See below, p. 121.

maximum was fixed at twelve. Workers were entitled to the public holidays provided for by the Government (seven a year), and to any other customary vacations. Rest periods and leave were to be continued according to 'the usual professional practice unless circumstances call for an adjustment to be made in collective agreements'. The articles on labour discipline included provisions for penalization and dismissal provided this was not contrary to any government law or decree, or to the existing collective agreement. Existing labour-welfare facilities were to be continued, including compensation for injury and disability.

The stabilization of wages in real terms through the wage-point system was adopted in all industrial and commercial enterprises, both state-operated and private, in the early years of the régime. The regulations provided that 'in order to avoid any possible effects of the variation of prices on wages, the local People's Government will publish a unified standard for calculating wages, based on the price index or on the current prices of a certain number of commodities'. Provision was also made for equal pay for equal work.

A procedure for the settlement of labour disputes was set out. This applied to public and co-operative, as well as privately operated, enterprises. It provided for direct consultation between workers and employers, if necessary with the assistance and participation of the higher organizations of workers and employers in the locality. It included recourse to the local labour office at the request of either party for conciliation, or, as an ultimate resort, for arbitration.

The Trade Union Law,[1] passed on 29 June 1950, laid down the structure and organization to be adopted by the unions. The law purported to put into effect the labour policy contained in the Common Programme. This envisaged a system under which workers would participate in the management of nationalized enterprises, in the determination of conditions of work in privately owned enterprises, and in the formation of trade unions under the leadership of the All-China Federation of Trade Unions.

[1] *Labour Laws and Regulations of the People's Republic of China* (Peking, Foreign Languages Press, 1956), p. 5.

Under the law all manual and non-manual workers employed by enterprises, institutions, and schools, for whom wages are their sole or main support, and all wage-earners without specific employers, are accorded the right to organize trade unions. It is laid down that trade unions must be organized according to the principle of democratic centralism (i.e. units at the lower level elect representatives to, and are in turn subordinate to, units at the higher level), in accordance with the Constitution of the All-China Federation of Trade Unions, and that they are to be formed into a nation-wide independent and united body, with the All-China Federation of Trade Unions as its principal organ. All trade unions, immediately upon being organized, must report to the All-China Federation of Trade Unions, or its affiliated industrial or local unions, and these bodies will consider and approve their establishment and register them with the appropriate People's Government organ. This is an indispensable condition of acceptance as an official trade union. Thus, from the very beginning, the Government made certain that unions could only exist with the official sanction of the local government organ, and that they should all be subordinate to the All-China Federation, which is of course effectively under the control of the Government. In practice, therefore, workers do not possess the opportunity to organize themselves spontaneously into representative organizations; unions are formed only under official auspices and under official control, exercised ultimately through the Communist Party organization.

The law specified the organization to be adopted by the individual unions. Factories, mines, shops, farms, institutions, schools, and other administrative or productive units with twenty-five or more workers and staff members are empowered to set up a 'primary trade union committee' (the factory, mine, institution, &c., committee). Full-time trade union officials are to be paid by the trade union at rates not lower than their original wages, and continue to share in labour insurance and other welfare schemes paid for by the management or the owner.

The sources of trade union income are membership dues of trade unionists, contributions from managements or owners, who must give to the trade unions each month a sum equal to 2 per cent. of the total real wages bill of all manual and non-manual workers employed (three-quarters of this amount is to be used on cultural and educational work for the workers), income from cultural and physical training undertakings sponsored by the trade unions, and subsidies from the People's Governments at various levels. Under the Trade Union Law, trade unions are to enjoy independence in their budgets, balance sheets, and auditing of accounts. Despite this assurance, general oversight of the finances of the trade union movement is entrusted to the All-China Federation of Trade Unions, which thus possesses another effective lever for control over the individual unions.

In China social insurance is administered through the trade unions. The regulations on Labour Social Insurance, adopted in March 1952,[1] expanded the social-insurance clauses of the Trade Union Law into a comprehensive system of benefits, payable to different classes of workers on varying scales. During periods of sickness benefits of 60–100 per cent. of wages (if the sickness or accident has occurred through work) are paid, and the cost of hospitalization, doctors, and medicine is to be paid by the employer. Retirement pensions of 50–70 per cent. of average wage (at 60 for men, 50 for women), death benefit of 2–3 months' wages, and maternity benefit of full wages for 56–70 days are also paid. About 9 million workers are at present covered by the social-insurance regulations.

The Constitution for Trade Unions promulgated on 10 May 1953[2] described the tasks of the unions as to

strengthen the unity of the working class, to consolidate the alliance of workers and peasants, to educate the workers to observe consciously the laws and decrees of the state and labour discipline, to strive for the development of production, for the constant increase of labour productivity, for the fulfilment and over-fulfilment of the production plans of the state. . . .

They were called upon actively to improve 'the material and cultural life of the workers'. This Constitution, of which a revised version was published in December 1957, gives some

[1] *Labour Laws and Regulations of the People's Republic of China* (Peking, Foreign Languages Press, 1956), p. 31.   [2] Ibid., p. 16.

idea of some of the subsidiary functions performed by the unions. These include the provision of cultural and educational activities, the organization of savings, the supervision of safety precautions, and the running of recreational and welfare facilities, including dormitories and public kitchens. Such activities may well represent the most important, indeed perhaps the only important, tasks performed by the unions on behalf of the individual worker.

A tightening in the attitude of the Government towards labour was heralded by the adoption by the State Administrative Council, on 6 May 1954, of 'The Outline of Labour Regulations for State-Operated Enterprises'. This Order laid special emphasis on the need for labour discipline, and for an increase in labour productivity to match the expanding targets of the Five-Year Plan. This stiffening of attitude perhaps represented the impact of the mounting demands of the industrialization programme on the working population. Early in 1954 it was reported that political and legal departments of the Peking Municipal Government were co-operating in 'further measures to ensure the smooth progress of State economic construction and socialist reform'. A special tribunal was established in Peking to handle a new category of crimes, 'economic offences', covering a wide range from 'sabotage' to negligence. Three work teams were sent to selected industrial areas to make inquiries and establish 'key points for political and legal work'. A special court and a special prosecutors' office were set up for Peking Railways, and national bodies, such as the Central Political and Legal Committee, the Ministry of Justice, the Supreme People's Court, and the People's Procurator General's Office encouraged similar activities on the part of other municipal authorities. By the summer of 1954 the Supreme People's Procurator, together with the Deputy Procurator-General, had been put in charge of a widespread system of punishment for workers found guilty—usually by so-called 'comrade tribunals' —of neglecting or 'sabotaging' production; workers were sent to prison for a wide variety of offences such as negligence, absenteeism, mismanagement of materials, and failure to observe operational regulations.

With the inauguration of the Five-Year Plan and the

accompanying nationalization of industry, trade unions became increasingly used to popularize and to implement government policy (for example, in taking the correct stand on problems arising over the industrialization programme, and carrying on propaganda for the established wage system) in the industrial field. The emphasis has been more and more on productivity and discipline; Soviet methods, such as labour emulation campaigns (i.e. production competitions), bulletin and notice-board citations, and the maximum possible publicity to improve labour performance and industrial relations, have been widely used for these ends.

It is evident that many trade union members themselves are not only well aware of the unrepresentative nature of the Chinese trade unions, but thoroughly dissatisfied with them. A remarkably frank article in the *People's Daily* in August 1957 described a 2,500-mile tour by the Deputy Head of the General Office of the All-China Federation of Trade Unions, accompanied by a member of the Chinese Government. They visited ten cities from Peking to Canton. Some of the trade union members in Canton complained that the union officials were hand-in-glove with the administration. In Canton, Changsha, Wuhan, and other places the trade unions were known as 'the tongues of the bureaucracy, and the tails of the administration and the workers' control department'. It was said that trade union officials never really devoted themselves to fighting for the workers' interests. Sometimes working conditions were found to be appalling—excessive hours were worked and workers were being driven too hard—but the trade unions had done nothing to help. In subsequent correspondence, some trade union officials complained that if they did try to do what they could for the workers, they got no response from state officials and might be regarded by these as trouble-makers or as 'tailists'.

Perhaps partly to remedy the frustration among the workers caused by this situation, the Government during 1956 and 1957 did make some efforts to ensure some sense of participation by the workers in the affairs of the enterprises for which they worked. In a speech to the CP Congress in September 1956 Li Hsueh-feng suggested that workers' and employers' conferences for particular enterprises (something on the lines of a joint production committee in Britain) should be set up in which workers would be allowed to criticize the management of the enterprise and put forward proposals. In March 1957 Lai Jo-yu, then head of the trade union organization, made a speech recommending the introduction of a system of 'democratic management' in industry through the formation of 'workers' representative conferences', which would have the right to recommend appointments and dismissals of the management staff, to discuss and criticize production plans and make their own proposals. In March experiments on these lines were instituted in five organizations in different parts of the country. It was admitted that previously the participation of the workers had been of a consultative rather than executive character; in practice, the managing director had absolute power, and there had been rigid direction from above. The new system was designed to remedy this.

It was said that in the Peking Tram Company, a state enterprise, a workers' representative conference of 191 representatives elected by the workers had formed a new 'administrative committee' of nineteen for the Company, including representatives of the workers, management, technicians, CCP, trade unions, and Youth League, but 'with a majority of workers'. This was elected for a period of a year, and was said to have power to elect the managing director and assistant managing directors, to study and decide on the Company's plans for production, technical measures, and finance, to supervise the carrying out of state policies and directives, to investigate and decide on systems of organization, rules and regulations, labour safety, wages, promotion, awards and penalties, &c. In Mukden a slightly less radical system was tried, in which the director and leading officials continued to be appointed by the state, though, should any of them prove incompetent, the representative conference had the right to criticize and if necessary propose to higher authority that the official concerned should be removed.

The system of representative meetings and of 'blooming and contending' discussions, in which factory workers were encouraged to engage in public criticism of factory managements, was officially sanctified in the preamble to the revised Constitution for Trade Unions adopted in December 1957. But it is likely that in practice local Communist Parties will ensure that any representative body is dominated by Party members or their sympathizers. In May 1957 the Mukden Communist Party committee, reporting on the Mukden experiment as it affected the Communist Party, said that no matter how far democracy was extended in the factories, the leading administrative personnel should have full responsibility for production. The CCP factory committee should therefore intensify political and ideological education among the workers so that the representative conferences would not interfere with the administrative work of the enterprises: 'party organs and trade unions should encourage the workers to adhere to the rules and regulations of the enterprises and to listen to the instructions of the leading administrative personnel'.

By 1958 the total number of 'wage-earners' had reached 25 million. About half of these are employed in industry, building, transport, and communications; so that probably not more than about 3–4 million are factory workers. The other half are presumably clerks, shop assistants, and other urban workers.

It is fairly clear, however, that despite this rapid increase, there is still a good deal of unemployment in the towns. From the earliest days of the régime there have been complaints by the authorities about what is described as the 'blind movement of peasants to the towns'. This probably results from the ever-increasing pressure of the rapidly growing agricultural population on the available land resources, the desire of some of the peasant population to share the rising standard of living of the urban workers, and perhaps also from dissatisfaction among some of the peasantry with the effects of land reform and collectivization. At various times fairly drastic steps have been taken to hold and even to reverse the movement; for example, peasant immigrants to Shanghai have been rounded up and sent back to their villages.

Such measures cannot, however, remedy the fundamental causes of unemployment, which arise from the fact that, while the Chinese population is increasing at an annual rate of about

12–15 million, urban employment is apparently rising by not much more than a million a year. An article in the *People's Daily* in November 1957 admitted that only a part of available Chinese manpower could be absorbed in industry in spite of its rapid expansion. For this reason determined efforts should be made to open employment opportunities in other fields. For example, agriculture ought to be able to absorb more people; if every co-operative took five more members, 3·75 million would find work. The 'surplus population of the cities' should be encouraged to go to the countryside and the 'hilly areas', to take part in agriculture or forestry. Housewives should learn to content themselves with housework which was 'as honourable' as any other kind of work. More attention must be paid to the possibility of increasing employment in the service trades, the catering business, handicraft co-operatives, and other forms of ancillary work.

In November 1957, probably largely as a result of the growing difficulties over unemployment, new provisional regulations on retirement were published. Under these regulations, male workers were to retire at 60 and female workers at 50 if they had worked continuously for five years before. The retiring age would be five years earlier for those who had worked in mines, and places where altitude or pressure was high. Normally retirement pay was to be 50 per cent. of wages for those who had worked more than five years and less than ten years, 60 per cent. for those who had worked ten to fifteen years, and 70 per cent. for those who had worked fifteen years or more. The measure is thus likely to have a strongly inflationary effect, and this fact alone is an indication of the measure of the Government's concern with the unemployment situation.

Apprenticeship schemes have been introduced in most Chinese industries and crafts. At first intensive courses of a year or eighteen months were introduced, and there was rapid promotion for those who had completed their apprenticeship. These methods, however, gave rise to difficulties, not only because of the failure of the apprentices to acquire a wide enough working knowledge of their trade, but also because of frictions in labour relations: apparently many young apprentices of 18 had felt themselves entitled to start ordering about older workers of far greater knowledge and experience. In 1957 new regulations were introduced providing for the extension of apprenticeship periods to three years, beginning at the minimum age of 16. After the completion of their course they were to be paid for the first year at the lowest possible rate, and afterwards would receive only gradual promotion according to the quality of their work.

Materially the industrial worker is probably in many ways better off than in earlier times. More is provided for him in the way of welfare and recreational facilities. Probably more attention is given to safety precautions and health measures. And he almost certainly receives higher wages in terms of purchasing power than his predecessors did. But the standards are still extremely low by Western standards. Though it is difficult to obtain clear evidence about wages, it seems that an average wage for a skilled industrial worker is somewhere about 80 or 90 yuan, which at the present rate of exchange is about £11 10s. 0d.–£13 a month, while a semi-skilled worker may get only about half this amount. This comparison is virtually meaningless, however. The Chinese worker will probably have free or very cheap housing: according to Chinese official figures, the average worker spends 3·5 per cent. of his income on rent. Simple Chinese food of the sort to which he is accustomed is fairly cheap, and so also is the type of clothing (blue denim battle-dress), now almost universally worn by Chinese men and women alike. On the other hand many articles which are objects of everyday use in working-class houses in Western countries are either very expensive or completely unobtainable in China.

In the middle of 1956 a wage increase averaging 14·5 per cent. was granted by the Government. The decision was said to have been reached after discussions with workers and trade unions, managements, and government departments. The minister responsible criticized himself for the fact that over the last two years wage increases had not been commensurate with the rise in productivity, and declared that the authorities would make sure that this did not happen again. The effect of the changes was to increase the differential for skill. There was a particularly large increase for teachers and administrative workers. There was an extension of the use of piece-work and the system of reward bonuses was 'improved'; and there was to be a special bonus where the cost of living was higher.[1]

The Chinese industrial worker has until recently, as in Russia, been paid almost entirely by piece-rates. This system, incompatible with true Communism, is apparently permissible in the transitional stage of socialism. During the last half of 1958, however, there has been a movement, especially in the communes, for a return towards payment on a time basis. In most industries in China, as in the Soviet Union and Eastern Europe, there are eight grades, varying according to the skill of the worker, each having different rates for piece-payments. Workers within the same industry may be promoted from one grade to another and this helps to prevent an excessive labour turnover. The rate for each grade varies from one industry to another, at government direction, according to the importance attached to the industry and the need to attract labour.

A six-day week is worked and there are normally no holidays other than the seven 'legal holidays' corresponding to British bank holidays. Workers in key industries, such as coal miners, have recently been working, in addition, on Sundays and even on some of the legal holidays.

Trade unionists are left in no doubt that they are not expected to make use of their organization in order to acquire any political influence for their members, or indeed to show any independence of action in any field. They are to remain in all things subject to the authority of the Communist Party. 'Trade unions must accept the leadership of the Party. This is the first rule of Heaven', Lai Jo-yu, the former government-appointed chief of the trade unions, has said. 'It is not permissible to express dissatisfaction with the Party either openly among the members

[1] In Nov. 1957 the Government announced that the future wage-rates of workers newly taken on in certain types of unskilled jobs were to be reduced. This was because of the unfavourable comparisons being made by the peasants between their own incomes and those of workers in these grades (see below, p. 188) which, in addition to creating discontent, were inducing them to flow into the cities in large numbers, 'causing additional employment difficulties'. Thus in future newly engaged 'ordinary workers', i.e. labourers, construction workers, &c., should not be paid 'unreasonably' highly in relation to the local peasants, but should receive about the same as an average peasant of a medium-size co-operative, plus whatever was justified by the difference of the cost of living between the cities and the rural areas. Newly engaged 'miscellaneous workers', i.e. clerks, railwaymen, busmen, servicing personnel, &c., were not to be paid more than the thirtieth grade wage in the current wage scale.

or at trade union meetings.'[1] This gives a fairly clear indication of the Government's conception of the role of the unions in Chinese society.

Nor is it likely that the trade unions exert much influence behind the scenes. Lai Jo-yu, who, until his death in 1958, controlled them, was a comparatively junior member of the Communist hierarchy (he came fifty-seventh in the list of the Central Committee of the CCP). There is no influential committee of the All-China Federation of Trades Unions like the General Council of the TUC, which might make its weight felt within the Government. The unions will therefore probably continue, as in the past, to be used largely as agents of government policy, as organs through which the Communist Party may wield influence over the working population, as administrators of welfare schemes, and as propagandists for encouraging the attainment of the highest possible production levels.

[1] Lai Jo-yu, *Trade Union Work Experience at the Wu-san Factory* (Peking, 1953), p. 21.

XI

FOREIGN TRADE

AFTER the foundation of the People's Republic, foreign trade quickly became virtually a state monopoly. In the early years control was by the Ministry of Trade. In August 1952 this was split into the Ministry of Internal Commerce and the Ministry of Foreign Trade. Overseas trade is now supervised and controlled by the Ministry of Foreign Trade and administered by twelve state companies covering the main divisions of foreign trade and the main products for export. This system gives the Government complete power to control the direction and volume of foreign trade according to the needs of the national economic programme. In 1950 official agencies controlled 70 per cent. of imports and 54 per cent. of exports. By 1953, 92 per cent., by 1954, 97 per cent., and by 1955, 99·2 per cent. of total trade was carried on by state enterprises.

Foreign trade is planned annually as part of the development of the Five-Year Plan. Normally, all trade is conducted on a barter basis. Long-term agreements within the Soviet *bloc* are based on the rouble as the unit of account and clearing, although delivery prices are, or can be, expressed in the currency of the supplying country; payments not concerning commercial transactions can also be included in the clearing, so long as the two central banks involved agree. Since January 1949 a Council of Mutual Economic Aid has existed in Moscow, charged with the task of co-ordinating the economic plans (and therefore the trading relationships) of the Soviet *bloc*. China is not a member of this Council, but sends observers to its meetings.

With Western countries normal commercial methods were used by the Chinese Government up to the outbreak of the Korean War in 1950. Purchases were paid for on receipt of documents, after the merchandise had been loaded or put on ship. But after 1950, when cargoes were sometimes intercepted *en route* to China by Nationalist warships and particularly after

May 1951, when the United Nations agreed to the embargo of 'strategic' exports to China, the Chinese Government adopted the use of letters of guarantee, which were promises on the part of a Chinese bank, generally the Bank of China, to pay for imports after they had been unloaded and inspected in a Chinese port. For exports the Government demanded payment immediately on the deposit of documents of ownership with the importers.

Agreements with Western countries recognizing the new Government could be either official, as with Finland and India, or non-official, like the one made with a British delegation representing industrial and exporting interests. Agreements with countries not recognizing the new Government, such as France, were not official, and were signed on the Chinese side by the Chinese Committee for the Promotion of International Trade, a body created on 4 May 1952, after the International Economic Conference held in Moscow in April 1952. The Sino-Japanese agreement of May 1955, however, was signed for China by official representatives, although Japan had not recognized the new Government and the Japanese signatories represented unofficial bodies.

The unit of account for Chinese trade with Western countries, and to an increasing extent the unit of payment, is the pound. China was accorded membership of the 'transferable-account' system, evolved by the United Kingdom as a step towards the multilateralization of payments, under the Nationalist Government. The Communist Government has continued to benefit from the increased volume of trade that membership has made possible. To the barter trade, which is still the rule, have been added a series of exchanges involving clearing agreements using the pound as a unit of account and payment.

China's foreign trade is an instrument of government economic policy, and its development has been geared closely to the development of the Five-Year Plan. Accordingly, during recent years, its chief function has been to foster the growth of heavy industry. In 1950 tariffs were imposed which discriminated in favour of industrial imports. Moderate rates, or exemption, from import tax were granted for imports of industrial equipment, raw materials, and for imports considered essential to the Government's economic programme, while highly protective rates were put on other goods, especially articles domestically produced. There was also discrimination in favour of countries already having commercial agreements with China.

In terms of 1952 prices the maximum value of China's foreign trade in the pre-war period was about $1,000 million. In 1958 the value had increased to over $4,500 million (at current prices at official rates of exchange). According to official figures, the balance of imports and exports has not been in deficit since 1950. This has been achieved through the bilateral trading policy adopted by the Government and the virtual state monopoly of trade.

The Chinese balance of payments has been considerably assisted by remittances from overseas Chinese. Efforts have been made by the Government to foster these by offering specially advantageous terms, both as to interest rates and security, for the investment of such funds in mainland China. The Government have established an Overseas Chinese Investment Company, which pays an interest of 8 per cent. on funds invested by overseas Chinese, and builds with them industrial establishments (sugar refineries, oil presses, resin mills, &c.), mainly in Fukien, the home province of many overseas Chinese. Recently investment has principally been in co-operative and joint state-private enterprises. The authorities have been careful to reassure overseas investors that their investments, unlike those of investors in China, will not be affected by socialization, and that any remittances they make to their families will be protected and may be used 'either for investment or for personal livelihood'. China also acquires substantial sums of foreign exchange as a result of her trade with Hong Kong and Macao.

There has been a considerable change in the direction of Chinese foreign trade since 1949, and particularly since the start of the Korean War. Chinese trade with the Soviet Union and the 'People's Democracies' has increased by more than seven times between 1950 and 1958, and as a proportion of total trade has increased from 26 per cent. in 1950 to about 80 per cent. in 1958. Its total value was then thought to be over $3,500 million a year at official rates of exchange. Trade with the West (including non-Communist Asian countries) now amounts to nearly $1,000 million, not much more than before the war, but the proportion has declined from nearly three-quarters to a fifth of the total. The volume is, however, rising, and in 1956 was over 25 per cent. more than in 1955, while trade with the Soviet *bloc* rose by only 1·5 per cent. in that year. About three-quarters of this total is with Asian and African countries, especially Malaya, Ceylon (who both supply rubber), Japan, and Pakistan. Among Western countries Western Germany has now regained her pre-war dominance, with Switzerland and the United Kingdom not far behind.

British Trade with China

(£ million sterling)

	1955	1956	1957
British imports	12·30	12·55	14·23
British exports (incl. re-exports)	7·97	10·78	12·94

Source: Board of Trade

Within the Soviet *bloc*, China's principal trading partner is, of course, the Soviet Union, from which she obtains all kinds of machinery, petrol, chemicals, tractors and motor vehicles, and some raw materials. Among other Communist countries the trade with East Germany and Czechoslovakia, the two most industrially advanced countries, is probably the most important, and China has become an important market for East German and Czech engineering and machinery exports. Trade with Poland is also considerable. Polish deliveries consist chiefly of machine tools, mining and farm machinery, iron and steel products and non-ferrous metals; and complete plants in the form of two sugar refineries have been supplied. Poland also has the important role within the Sino-Soviet *bloc* of shipping exchanges of goods between Eastern Europe and China, thus relieving the strain on the overland route. Hungary supplies various types of equipment, machine tools, locomotives and lorries, in which she specializes. Trade contacts have also been made with Rumania (which supplies oil-drilling equipment) and Bulgaria (which sends artificial fertilizers and chemicals).

There is, in addition, a growing two-way exchange of technical missions between China and the satellite countries. A permanent Chinese purchasing mission covering Eastern Europe was established in East Berlin in 1952.

Over recent years there has been an expansion of trade with non-Communist countries. Already, by the end of 1954, trade relations had been established with over sixty countries. In particular, there has been a big increase in trade with South East Asia, which has included the export by China of light industrial products.

Chinese efforts to develop their trade with South East Asia and especially with Hong Kong, Singapore, and Indonesia, were suddenly intensified during 1958 at the beginning of the second Five-Year Plan. Consumer goods such as textiles, bicycles, shoes, cameras, sugar, and other foodstuffs were loaded on to the market at prices so low that they undercut even Japanese and Hong Kong producers. Sometimes these exports included goods which were known to be in short supply in China itself, such as cement, cotton cloth, footwear, and sugar (which was being imported from Indonesia). Sometimes the choice of exports seemed to have some political significance, for example to create economic difficulties for Japan, with which China was then conducting a trade war, or for Formosa, whose exports of cement and sugar were seriously affected. But the principal object was almost certainly to acquire new supplies of foreign exchange, badly needed to finance the purchases of steel and other capital equipment that the Chinese authorities were at that time making in the West.

Throughout the first years of the régime, Chinese trade with non-Communist countries was carried out almost entirely by Western shipping companies. During 1958, however, apparently as a result of differences over freight rates, the Chinese chartered, mainly in Western Europe, over 100 ships for trading purposes. In addition they purchased a small number of liberty-type merchant ships, which were taken over by Chinese crews. It seems likely that in the future an increasing proportion of China's trade with the West (and possibly with the Soviet *bloc* as well) will be carried by Chinese-owned or Chinese-controlled shipping.

The composition of Chinese trade has also changed a good deal since 1949. Before the war imports were principally of consumer commodities, for example textiles and foodstuffs. Grain imports ceased in 1950 (although they were resumed temporarily in 1954 with some rice imports from Burma). In 1951 and 1952 China exported sizeable quantities of grain, particularly to India, and there has been a regular export of rice to Ceylon in exchange for rubber. A good deal of grain is also exported to Russia to pay for industrial imports. Exports of grain and soya beans to Russia and other countries are believed to amount to about 3 million tons a year. Textile requirements are now virtually satisfied by domestic production, though there are still small imports of raw cotton from Egypt and Pakistan.

The main emphasis in the Chinese import programme today is, of course, on imports of capital goods and industrial raw materials. In 1953 and 1954 the share of these categories in total imports was 89 per cent.; in trade with the Soviet *bloc* the proportion was 93·5 per cent., and with the Soviet Union alone 97 per cent. In that year 93·9 per cent. of total capital imports came from the Soviet *bloc*. Beginning in 1953, with the start of the Five-Year Plan, the import from the Soviet *bloc* of complete sets of equipment for installation in factories has been common, together with imports of machine tools, precision instruments, mining machinery, transport equipment, cranes, vehicles, rolled steel, non-ferrous metals, electrical and tele-communications equipment, and raw materials for the chemical industry. The principal imports from non-Communist countries are rubber, fertilizers, and other chemicals.

In recent years some imports have been made for light industry, e.g. cotton, cured tobacco, jute and wool tops for higher-grade woollen fabrics. Imports of draught animals, agricultural machinery, high-grade seed, and considerable quantities of chemical fertilizer were also provided for in the Five-Year Plan, as part of the effort to boost agricultural output. Imports of consumer commodities have consisted chiefly of sugar, special-type textiles, paper, kerosene oil, and medical supplies.

Chinese exports remain largely the traditional ones of

agricultural, mineral, and native products. About half the volume of exports at present consists of foodstuffs. An export programme along these lines was drawn up for the first Five-Year Plan period. Typical exports to the Soviet *bloc* are rice, tea, silks, hides, feeding-stuffs, egg products, soya beans, tungsten, wolfram and other rare metals, tung-oil, tobacco, bristles, feathers, animal products, and, recently, textiles. Among the principal exports to the West are feeding-stuffs, oil-seeds, and soya beans.

Beginning in 1954 various new types of exports of light industrial goods have appeared, e.g. cotton textiles, which before the war were imported, bicycles, and electrical apparatus. In that year, also, China exported capital equipment for the first time, with the dispatch of steel strips and steel constructional equipment to Burma and Egypt. This trend was continued in the Sino-Indonesian trade agreement, which envisages Chinese exports of machine tools, textile machinery, and other industrial equipment. Exports today are said to include machinery and equipment for textile, paper, and cement factories, rolled-steel machine tools, diesel engines, rubber tyres, wireless sets, sewing machines, and woollen textiles.

In the last few years efforts have been made by some Western countries, including the United Kingdom, to expand their trade with China, though for long they were limited in this by the embargo on the export of strategic goods to that country. The British efforts, partly sponsored by the Federation of British Industries, were designed, not only to encourage trade but to reorientate it into normal commercial channels. Chinese trade delegations visited the United Kingdom in 1954 after the Geneva Conference, in 1957, and again in 1958. Several delegations of British business men visited China from 1953 onwards. In October 1957 Mr. Erroll, the Parliamentary Secretary to the Board of Trade, paid a visit to China, the first official visit by a member of the British Government since the start of the régime, and in the next month an important Chinese technical mission came to Britain to discuss trading possibilities. Chinese technical groups have also visited France and other countries. But the Chinese have always been primarily interested in the purchase of strategic goods, all of which were once and some of which are still on the embargo list.

As a result of her inability to purchase abroad the goods she was principally interested in, China accumulated during this period a substantial surplus with most Western countries. She had a surplus with the sterling area of £40 million in 1955 and £67 million in 1956. In mid-1957 her sterling balances were believed to be about £100 million.[1] This balance was partly used to finance trade with other countries in the transferable account area, including the Soviet Union. But the Chinese were probably holding some of it in reserve until such time as the embargo was lifted.

Thus the embargo, administered by COCOM (the Consultative Group Co-ordinating Committee) in Paris, has for long been the principal factor restricting Chinese trade with most Western countries. Initiated as a result of Chinese intervention in the Korean War, it was maintained with only slight modifications for several years after the conclusion of the war, and was more stringent than the restrictions placed on exports to other Soviet *bloc* countries. In May 1957, after discussion in COCOM the British Government announced that they intended to abandon the differential between the Soviet and China lists. This example was later followed by most of the other members of COCOM. Goods freed by this move included most motor vehicles and tractors, railway locomotives and rolling stock, iron and steel, aluminium and copper products, some machine tools, electric motors and generators, raw rubber, tyres and some chemicals; but a limiting quota was retained for some of these goods.

In July 1958 there was a further relaxation of the new joint list for the Soviet *bloc*. Most types of machine tool, motor-cars and lorries not built to military specification, civil aircraft, aero engines, electrical equipment, most forms of petrol and most types of ship were freed. As a result of this move, considerable Chinese orders were placed in Western Europe for textile machinery, copper wire, motor vehicles, electrical equipment, and other goods. The United States Government, although they, somewhat reluctantly, agreed to these changes, continue to prevent any trade at all with China by United States enterprises.

---

[1] *The Economist*, 8 June 1957, p. 912.

There are differences of opinion on how far it may be possible to increase Western trade with China as a result of these relaxations. Since the embargo was modified, and especially during 1958, the Chinese have been placing fairly large orders in the United Kingdom and other Western countries. British exports to China increased by 13 per cent. during 1957, and the prospects of further growth were said by Mr. Erroll to be 'quite good'. It certainly seems possible that the Chinese may seek so far as possible to relieve themselves of a small part of the burden of their agricultural exports to the Soviet Union by obtaining from the West any capital equipment that is obtainable there, and for which they can afford to pay in Western currencies.

One limiting factor in expanding Chinese trade with the West, as with other countries, in the immediate future, may be China's capacity to increase her exports. Many of the raw materials that were traditionally exported, such as iron and coal, will now be fully required for China's own industries (though the Chinese were at one time reported to have been attempting to revive their pre-war exports of iron to Japan). Their rapidly increasing population will continue to absorb most, if not all their agricultural production. And demand for such old-style exports as bristles, sesame oil, feathers, silk, and hides is limited; though cheap consumer goods, such as textiles, shoes, gloves, bicycles, and so on may, like those produced in Hong Kong, prove strongly competitive in many Western markets, as they have already done in South East Asia.

In the longer term it seems likely that, with the expansion of the Chinese economy, there may be room for an increase in trade all round, and especially with non-Communist countries. Although the Chinese Government are making a big effort to increase their self-sufficiency, there will certainly be a continuing Chinese demand for machinery and specialized types of capital equipment. Cheap Chinese labour costs will give Chinese goods a strong position in export markets as the country's industrial capacity develops. At the same time, absorption of Chinese exports by Soviet-*bloc* countries may have reached, or may be about to reach, saturation point: Chinese exports to Eastern European countries are sometimes resold at competitive prices to Western Europe. And the Chinese themselves will probably not be sorry to diversify the sources of their imports, especially if they are able to obtain capital goods in exchange.

But it will be some time before industrial exports can be developed on any scale. Until that happens, the basis of Chinese trade with the outside world will probably remain the exchange of agricultural and mineral products for machinery and capital equipment.

THE DEVELOPMENT OF AGRICULTURE

XII

LAND REFORM

THE Chinese Communist revolution differed from all other Communist revolutions which have taken place so far in that it depended for its success largely on support from the agricultural population. The leaders of the CCP early recognized the need for this support. In a famous passage of an early work Mao Tse-tung wrote that, if ten points were allotted for the accomplishment of the democratic revolution, the urban dwellers and military units rated only three points, while the other seven should go to the peasants.[1] Agrarian reform, that is the redistribution of land, has therefore occupied a particularly important position in the programme of the Chinese Communists, and was regarded as a primary task once the revolution had been accomplished. Reform of the system of land tenure in China of one sort or another had in fact often been recommended by many who were not communists or even left-wing (a land reform measure has now been introduced even by the Nationalist régime in Formosa). For the communists the introduction of such a measure was inevitable, not only for the sake of the political advantages to be gained, but in order to conform with the political dogmas which they professed.

Before their assumption of power the policy of the Chinese Communists on land reform fluctuated at different times between the extremes of general redistribution and liquidation of landowners, carried out during the early years, to the comparatively mild practice of fixing 'economic rents', current during the 'united front' with the Nationalists in the Japanese War. When the civil war was resumed in 1946, the Communist Party issued a new directive authorizing the confiscation and redistribution of landlord property. Many poor peasants, however, demanded that the land of the rich peasants, part of

[1] *Report on the Investigation into the Agricultural Movement in Honan*, original Chinese edition, p. 22. This passage has been omitted from versions of the work published recently in Peking.

which was rented out, should also be included in the redistribution scheme. Ambiguity in the directive caused divergent practices in different areas, and for a time there was a good deal of confusion. A 'Basic Programme' was therefore put out in September 1947, extending the policy of confiscation to the 'surplus property' of rich peasants, and providing for equal distribution of land in exact ratio to population.

In the early days this campaign was marked by many excesses. Leagues of poor peasants were formed as the instruments of the redistribution process, and the movement was accompanied by much destruction and violence. Accusation meetings were called, virulent denunciations took place, summary judgements on dispossession and redistribution of property were enunciated; and frequently landlords were murdered. Arbitrary interpretations of the class definitions were made so that, for example, ordinary peasants were classified as 'rich peasants' and consequently deprived of much of their property.

By 1949 the Communist authorities evidently decided that some of these excesses would have to be curbed, if only to safeguard food production, to prevent disorder getting out of control, and to counter the discontent they were arousing among important sectors of the population. These considerations assumed even greater importance when they became responsible for the government of the whole country towards the end of that year. This development was reflected in the Common Programme, adopted in September 1949, which, while confirming peasant property rights in areas where land reform had already been put into effect, stipulated that in other areas the organization of the peasants and the revision of rents and interest rates should precede the actual distribution of land. The Government apparently wished to ensure that land reform should only take place under the supervision of their own officials, and to prepare more considered regulations governing the method of conducting the reform.

In 1949, on the eve of the main land-reform campaign, there was still considerable peasant ownership of land in China, although its distribution was unequal. It was estimated during the 1930's that at that time somewhere around half of the privately owned farm land was owned by the farmer himself.[1] Since these surveys were made, there had probably been some growth in tenancy, especially at the expense of part-ownership. This was a continuation of a trend noticed by Chinese economists earlier, which suggested an increase in land concentration, particularly in Manchuria, where commercial development was finding greater scope. Some of the privately owned land was held in large amounts by single landholders and leased to farmers, but the extent of farm tenancy in China was less than in many regions of Europe.[2] The holding of an average landlord was, moreover, only about 40 acres, and the pattern of distribution was quite different from that in the Soviet Union at the time of land reform there, where estates of anything up to 6,000 acres and more might be acquired for redistribution.

Some change of emphasis was apparent in the Agrarian Reform Law which was introduced in June 1950.[3] The law still described its aim as the abolition of the 'land ownership system of feudal exploitation', and called for the confiscation of land-owners' land, draught animals, farm implements, and 'surplus' grain, for distribution to landless and land-hungry peasants. But part of its object seems to have been to regularize the procedure to be observed, and to ensure that disorder and violence should not get out of control.

The law introduced a new system for determining the 'class status' of the different sections of the rural population. The rural population was divided into five categories: landlords, rich peasants, middle peasants, poor peasants, and workers or farm labourers. The rich peasants and middle peasants were subdivided into different categories, depending on how much land they cultivated themselves and how much they rented out, the degree of 'exploitation' indulged in, the number of farm labourers employed, and other considerations.

The most important change introduced by the new law was the exemption from confiscation of land belonging to rich peasants which was directly cultivated by them and their hired labour. It was also enacted that land rented out by a rich peasant, not exceeding the amount he and his workers tilled,

[1] See above, p. 7.
[2] Buck, *Land Utilization in China*, pp. 194, 196.
[3] *NCNA*, Suppl. No. 54, 30 June 1950.

could be retained by its owner. Even landlords were to keep their share of the redistributed land and, if they owned industrial or commercial enterprises, these too could be retained. Land cultivated by the owner and his own family was never to be drawn on for redistribution.

The result of such a measure was bound to be an unequal distribution of land. Not only were the initial units of land unequal, but the preservation under the law of rights of sale, purchase, and, on a restricted scale, of renting, made the emergence of further differentiation possible. The Agrarian Law was, in fact, concerned more with establishing the principle of peasant-proprietorship than with equalizing the size of holdings. Article 1 states categorically that 'the system of peasant land ownership shall be carried into effect'; and the rights of peasant-proprietorship were restated and formally guaranteed in Article 20 by the provision that, once land reform had been achieved, the People's Government should issue title-deeds and should recognize the rights of all landowners to manage, buy, sell, or rent out land freely. This recognition of the principle of private property by a Communist régime was justified in Article 1 of the law, where the private ownership of land was said to be intended to 'set free the rural productive forces, develop agricultural production and pave the way for the industrialisation of the new China'.

The law also gave official sanction to the continued use of hired labour. Thus there might still be some degree of stratification in the rural social structure; though in practice, since all peasants qualified for redistribution, it may not always have proved possible to find anybody willing to undertake work as a hired labourer.

That some protection was to be accorded to the wealthier peasants from the rapacity of envious neighbours is shown clearly in the procedure laid down in the law for the organization of the redistribution. The chief agency for redistribution was the peasant association, and one-third of the leadership of the associations had to come from the 'middle peasants', including the 'well-to-do' middle peasants. The determination of class status—an important part of the machinery of reform—was, according to Article 31, to be by 'democratic estimation and decision', and various safeguards were provided under this head. 'Democratic estimation' was carried out by village peasant meetings and peasants' representative gatherings organized by official *kanpus*. But their decisions had to be ratified by the People's Government at the county level (the unit of land-reform organization was the *hsiang*). Even then an appeal lay to the county People's Tribunal.

In a speech before the National Committee of the People's Political Consultative Conference, reported in *People's China* of 16 July 1950, Liu Shao-chi revealed the change in official thinking reflected in the new legislation. He explained that in the earlier stages of the civil war poor peasants had been allowed to take over the property of rich peasants in order to 'raise the peasants' revolutionary enthusiasm'. Once victory was assured 'the chief problems were those of finance and economy', and excesses formerly tolerated would no longer be permitted. Now that the Party was in power the basic aim of agrarian policy was not simply to relieve the lot of poor peasants, but to 'set free the rural productive forces'. Consequently, it was necessary to retain rich peasants and their economy within the framework of the reformed Chinese agriculture. The policy of peasant ownership would be maintained until conditions were ripe for the wider use of machinery in farming and for the organization of collective farms—until, that is, the 'socialist transformation' of the rural areas could be accomplished. In fact within the next six years, and long before there was any possibility of introducing any substantial degree of mechanization, most of the advantages to the peasant of owning his own holding had been cancelled out by the absorption of almost all peasant property in agricultural co-operatives.

In June 1950, when the law was published, land reform had already been accomplished in North China and other areas with a rural population of 145 million. The process of redistribution was then gradually extended southwards to remaining parts of the country. By February 1952 it had been carried out in areas with a population of over 310 million. By December 1952 it had been largely completed. The amount of land redistributed to landless peasants has never been exactly divulged, but seems to have varied from about 1 *mou* (one-sixth of an acre) per head in the east and south, where population densities are greatest, to 2–3 *mou* in central China, 3 *mou* in the north, and about 7 *mou* in north Manchuria.[1]

It is not clear whether the Government recognized at the time the land-reform campaign was being carried out how quickly the need to incorporate the tiny holdings into more economic units would make itself felt, and for how very short a space of time the peasants were in fact to be allowed to enjoy the unfettered use of their newly won holdings as individual proprietors. Although it is unlikely that the Communist leaders then envisaged collectivization being carried out so swiftly as, in the event, proved to be the case, they certainly knew that it would happen within the not too distant future. Thus while they made no secret of the necessity of eventual 'socialization', there was an element of hypocrisy in their campaign proclaiming the merits of a system of 'peasant land ownership'.

During the early stages of the land-reform campaign there was much violence, and there is no doubt that many injustices were committed. In many remote country areas the peasants, taking advantage of the Government's declared advocacy of land reform, seem to have taken the law into their own hands, and the process of redistribution then became the occasion for the wreaking of vengeance on unpopular landlords, and for the spoliation of the more prosperous peasants' land for the benefit of those less fortunate. In some cases they may have been directly encouraged in this by irresponsible local *kanpus*. Indeed the Government themselves lost no opportunity of stressing the importance of a relentless struggle to overthrow the landlord class. In some areas the process seems to have become entangled with the campaign against counter-revolutionaries, in which the authorities admit that about 2 million people were 'eliminated' (though this does not necessarily seem to have meant killed). In others the peasants are said to have spontaneously carried out the redistribution before the official procedure had been invoked.

At least in the later stages, however, the influence of the Government seems to have been directed towards moderating

[1] In a speech made on 23 Feb. 1957 Po I-po said that under the land reform 700 million *mou* of land had been distributed to 300 million peasants who formerly had little or no land.

the excesses which took place earlier, and preserving the rights of the richer peasants. This may have been in part the result of their recognition of the important role, both political and economic, of the rich-middle and rich peasant, so disastrously ignored in the Soviet Union, as well as of the need to preserve law and order in the countryside. Certainly some of the safeguards contained in the Land Reform Law itself, the elaborate instructions for the assessment of class status issued shortly afterwards, and the care taken to see that the reform should be undertaken only under the supervision of officials indicate that the authorities were seeking to ensure that the process should be accomplished without too great disorder, if not always without violence.

At the same time there must inevitably have been very severe social disturbances—the more severe in view of the sanctity in which the traditional social relationships had previously been held in China. These were probably intensified by the parallel upheavals which were taking place as a result of other government measures, such as the reform of the marriage system. All this must have exerted an extremely unsettling influence in the countryside, and there was as a result a considerable movement of country people towards the large towns, such as Shanghai.[1]

The reform may well also have had an unfavourable effect on agricultural production. Under the law, land was taken away from those who were probably marginally the more efficient producers and given instead to those who were if anything less efficient. At the same time, though the average size of a holding can have been little different from before, there were more very small units of land than ever. It may have been in part the recognition by the Government of the uneconomic nature of these units which hastened the introduction of the next phase of their agricultural policy.

[1] See above, p. 118.

XIII

THE COLLECTIVIZATION OF AGRICULTURE

THE Chinese authorities had from the earliest days declared that the 'collectivization' of agriculture was their final aim. But in the initial stages they gave the impression, at least in their public statements, that they were in no great hurry to bring about any sweeping changes in this direction, and that the progression towards their goal was thus likely to be a slow one. Article 34 of the Common Programme had stated that 'the People's Government . . . shall guide the peasants step by step to organize various forms of mutual aid, labour and production co-operation according to the principle of free choice and mutual benefits'. The first steps taken by the Government in the direction of collectivization seemed to be in conformity with this moderate programme.

In February 1951 the State Administrative Council, quoting Mao Tse-tung's words (from a speech made in June 1950) 'to get organized is the inevitable road from poverty to richness', called for the further development of 'mutual aid' in 'the old liberated areas' (where some form of mutual aid had been introduced since the early days of their administration by the Communists), and for its introduction in 'the new liberated areas'. This policy was set forth in a draft decision of the CCP Central Committee, formally proclaimed on 15 December 1952 and published on 26 March 1953.[1] A campaign was to be initiated to underline and demonstrate the economic advantages of co-operation and the pooling of resources. This was to be the second stage in the agrarian revolution (land reform having been the first), designed to enlarge the size of rural economic units and to create the foundation for the third stage, full-scale collectivization.

The three types of co-operative activity devised by the authorities as stages on the road to collectivization were

[1] *NCNA*, Suppl. No. 130, 2 Apr. 1953.

officially known as temporary mutual-aid teams; permanent mutual-aid teams; and semi-socialist agricultural producers' co-operatives. The final goal was the fully socialized co-operative, virtually the equivalent of the Russian collective farm.

In the temporary mutual-aid team, draught animals, tools, and the peasants' own labour were pooled or loaned for seasonal use, particularly for harvesting or sowing. This was merely a development of a practice already widespread in China, as in many other countries. In the permanent mutual-aid team this system was maintained as a permanent arrangement. Each member still retained full control over the use made of his own land, which continued to be worked as a separate unit. The unit of accounting was the 'work-day', and the standard work-day might consist of 10 points—2 for work in the early morning, 4 for work in the rest of the morning, and 4 for work in the afternoon. Ten points were the maximum any member could earn a day, depending on the amount and quality of his work. The work-day unit was in turn valued at a certain amount of grain, the value varying according to the type of work, e.g. ploughing, sowing, weeding, or harvesting. The actual method of payment was by 'point slips'. After the harvest, when the crops had been sold, the point slips were balanced in much the same way as cheques are cleared in a clearing house, and the net balance owing had to be paid in cash or kind or labour. The more expensive agricultural implements were bought for the team as a whole, each member contributing to the cost in proportion to the size of his holding. With the gradual accumulation of equipment, a flat-rate hiring charge was fixed for its use by members. As experience developed, the optimum size of a team was discovered to be about ten families.

In an agricultural producers' co-operative all the land was pooled and worked as a single unit. But each member retained his rights in his own land. He was credited with a certain number of shares, which entitled him to an ownership dividend according to the size of his contribution of land. A member of a co-operative was allowed, as in a Russian collective farm, to keep a plot of land for his personal use, for example for raising vegetables, fruit, or livestock (which he might market personally), and was also in theory free to withdraw his share of land from the co-operative. The system of payment for farm work was similar to that followed in mutual-aid teams. Out of the net produce of the co-operative a typical distribution was said to be 52 per cent. for wages, 40 per cent. for the dividend imputed to land, and 8 per cent. for 'public savings'.

In the higher stage or 'fully socialist co-operative', the return to the members out of the collective's profits was determined only by the labour each contributed. They received no payment for their land, though there would be compensation for the tools or animals which they had contributed to the farm. Each member might still retain a small plot for his own use. The organization was thus similar to that of the collective farm in Russia. In Russia, however, the land owned by a collective is the property of the state, and is made over to the collective under a charter on a semi-permanent basis. For this reason the members cannot, as they were supposed to be able to do in China, withdraw, taking their former land. There appear to have been no farms of this kind in China. There are, of course, state farms, worked by paid managers and labourers under the supervision of the Ministry of State Farms: these are often run as model farms for the co-operatives in the surrounding areas, and are on a far larger scale than the co-operatives (their average size is about 3,000–4,000 acres).

On 15 February 1952 the State Administrative Council published a decree on Agricultural Production for 1952, which for the first time set targets for the collectivization campaign. In the old liberated areas (those areas held by the Communists before the outbreak of the civil war in 1946), 80–90 per cent. of the peasants were to be organized in mutual-aid groups in the course of 1952 and 1953, while in the new liberated areas the work was to be accomplished in three years, i.e. by 1954, when all households should be attached to some kind of mutual-aid team, either temporary or permanent. Producer co-operatives were also to be developed in areas where there was a strong mutual-aid tradition. By the end of 1952 about 40 per cent. of the farm population were members of mutual-aid groups, but only one-quarter of 1 per cent. had joined agricultural producers' co-operatives.

In 1953 the co-operative campaign seems to have encountered its first difficulties. There was apparently some resistance by the peasantry, who were not unnaturally disposed to enjoy the benefits which land reform had conferred on them as individual landholders, to incorporation in co-operatives. These problems were experienced most sharply in Hopei, where co-operation was particularly advanced—1,082 of the 3,644 co-operatives existing in 1952 were in that province. Lin Tieh, provincial secretary for the Party in Hopei, in an account which appeared only in 1955, said that it was decided to dissolve over one-third of the total number of co-operatives in the province because of resistance from the peasants. This decision was later criticized as showing excessive caution, but shows clearly that peasant hostility was already fairly intense.

Despite this set-back, in October 1953 a national conference on mutual aid and co-operation in agriculture was summoned by the Central Committee of the Communist Party, and as a result it was decided to press forward with the development of agricultural producer co-operatives. At that time there were about 15,000 such co-operatives. The Party resolution stipulated that the number of co-operatives was to grow to 35,800 between the winter of 1953 and the autumn harvest of 1954. A target of 800,000 producer co-operatives by 1957, equivalent to 20 per cent. of all peasant households, was set for the first Five-Year Plan.

Producer co-operatives were formed rapidly in 1954, and the target originally set was quickly passed. By March 1954 there were already 91,000, representing 1,666,000 peasant households, or 1·43 per cent. of all peasant households. In the light of this development, the Central Committee of the CCP decided, in October 1954, to expand the number of co-operatives to over 600,000 before the spring sowing of 1955. Chou En-lai's report on government work, delivered at the First Session of the first National People's Congress on 25 September 1954, declared that in the course of the Five-Year Plan over half the peasant households and of the farm area would be absorbed in producer co-operatives. The work of expansion was thus continued during the winter of 1954–5 (the main activity in organizing co-operatives took place in the period between the autumn harvest and the spring sowing). By February the target of over 600,000 had been passed, and 670,000 co-operatives were reported to have been formed.

In March 1955 there was evidence that some doubts as to the wisdom of pressing on with the programme at quite such a break-neck speed were beginning to make themselves felt. The Decision on Spring Cultivation adopted by the State Administrative Council at its sixth meeting on 3 March 1955,[1] while noting the rapid growth of producer co-operatives, went on to observe that, because the co-operatives had been developed 'rather quickly' and without sufficient experience and preparation, a section of the peasants came to have 'suspicions and misunderstandings concerning the co-operative movement'. The movement must therefore be somewhat slowed down; the formation of new co-operatives should be stopped before the spring planting; and efforts should be concentrated on reorganizing the existing co-operatives to ensure their consolidation. Later a revised target of 33 per cent. of peasant households to be incorporated in agricultural producers' co-operatives by the end of 1957 was set in place of the 50 per cent. target published in the autumn of 1954.[2] A policy of contraction was initiated in Chekiang in April 1955, with the result that among 53,000 co-operatives then existing in that province 15,000 were disbanded at one stroke.[3] Similar action was taken at about the same time in Hopei and Shansi.

The confusion which appears to have existed at this time was not resolved until two national conferences of provincial party leaders for the discussion of agricultural co-operation had taken place in May and July 1955. The May conference stopped the policy of 'contraction', although it did not reverse the line completely. At the July conference Mao Tse-tung gave his report 'On Agricultural Co-operation', and set the stage for the spurt in co-operation which took place in the second half of 1955. This speech, which was not published until October 1955, when that year's harvest had been safely brought in and the new campaign was well under way, was a call to advance more

[1] BBC, Econ. Suppl. No. 1956, 24 Mar. 1955.
[2] Li Fu-chun's report to the National People's Congress in July 1955.
[3] Mao Tse-tung's report 'On Agricultural Co-operation', 31 July 1955 (*People's Daily*, 17 Oct. 1955).

quickly on the road to collectivization. At that time there were still only 15 million, out of a total of 110 million peasant households, already absorbed in agricultural producers' co-operatives.

Mao Tse-tung claimed that the great majority of peasants were eager to embark on the path of socialism, and that it was impossible to achieve socialist industrialization without the development of agricultural co-operatives. He called therefore for the inclusion of about 30 million peasant households, or double the number at that time, by spring 1956, and about 55 million peasant households, or half the rural population, by spring 1958. By 1960 the other half should have joined. But he demanded, in spite of this precise timetable, that the peasants should join only 'voluntarily'.

On 11 October 1955 a decision on the question of agricultural co-operation was adopted by the Central Committee of the CCP. This contained new targets for an even more rapid programme. In areas where mutual aid and co-operation were relatively advanced, 70–80 per cent. of all the local peasant households should have joined the producer co-operatives by the spring of 1957. In the majority of areas, where agricultural co-operatives included only about 10–20 per cent. of all peasant households in the spring of 1955, the same stage should be reached by the spring of 1958.

In the months which followed the announcement of this decision, various provincial committees published revised targets for co-operation within their provinces. These were considerably more ambitious than those set by the Central Committee and seemed to indicate that the target for the country as a whole had been put forward to 70–80 per cent. collectivization by 1956 for the advanced provinces, and a year later for the rest. Writing in the preface to *The Upsurge of Socialism in the Rural Areas of China*,[1] Mao Tse-tung declared: 'The next three or four years . . . will bring about the basic transition of the co-operatives from the semi-socialist stage to the fully socialist stage.'

In the early months of 1956 the movement even further accelerated. The draft Twelve-Year Plan for Agriculture, published in January 1956, demanded that the proportion of

[1] Peking, 1945; Mao's preface in *NCNA*, 12 Jan. 1956.

peasant households in agricultural producers' co-operatives should increase to 85 per cent. by the end of the year. Collectivization should be completed in the main by 1958. But by the middle of February, according to the *People's Daily* of 4 March 1956, there were already over 100 million peasant households, or 85 per cent. of the total, in co-operatives, while according to a directive on spring sowing issued by the State Administrative Council on 27 March 1956, the percentage of peasant households in co-operatives then had become 'over 90 per cent.'. By the end of 1956 it was announced that 96·1 per cent. of peasant households, farming 90 per cent. of the cultivated land, had joined the semi-socialist co-operatives, while 83 per cent. (compared with 4 per cent. at the end of 1955) or 100 million peasant households, had joined 500,000 'advanced co-operatives'.

The draft Plan for Agriculture[1] demanded that during 1956 steps should be taken to provide for the admission of former landlords and rich peasants to the co-operatives, if they wished. Those who had 'conducted themselves well' should be allowed to become full members of the local co-operative. Those who had 'conducted themselves fairly well' should be allowed to join as candidate members. Those who had shown themselves bad should continue under supervision, but would work for the co-operatives. If accepted as a member, a former landlord or rich peasant should be paid on an equal basis with the other members, but was not to occupy a post of importance within the co-operative.

One of the forms of pressure put on the peasant to join the co-operatives was an intensive propaganda campaign to persuade him that he would earn a higher income as a member of a co-operative. The Plan for Agriculture laid down as a condition for the establishment of co-operatives that 90 per cent. of the members should be able to earn higher incomes as a result of the change. In fact, in January 1957, it was admitted by a spokesman of the Ministry of Agriculture that this 'condition' had not been fulfilled, and that only about 70 per cent. of the peasants had higher incomes: and, since this is a standard which very easily lends itself to exaggeration, it is likely that the real figure may well be very much lower even than this.

[1] *NCNA*, Suppl. No. 236, 27 Jan. 1956. See below, p. 173.

It is fairly clear that this drop in income caused a good deal of discontent among those peasants who had previously been best off. Teng Tze-hui, the head of the department of the Rural Work of the Central Committee of the CCP, admitted[1] that some of the upper-middle peasants, accounting for about 5 per cent. of co-operative members, were dissatisfied because they found that production did not reach their own former production levels, and that some people even thought that 'the broad masses are dissatisfied over the co-operatives'. There was a substantial number of withdrawals from the co-operatives, especially in southern areas. In Kwangtung over 100,000 peasants withdrew, and 369 co-operatives had to be disbanded. It was declared that those farms which had been firmly based on the poor peasants had been able to resist the pressure for withdrawals, an interesting revelation of the class-orientated structure of most co-operatives and the true nature of the freedom to withdraw that is said to be assured.

By September 1957, 175 of the co-operatives dissolved in Kwangtung had been restored. But the authorities were clearly much concerned at the problem arising from the discontent of the wealthier peasants over lower incomes. In June and September new directives were issued calling on co-operatives to arrange their work schedules so as to benefit the previously better-off peasants, to pay extra income for work tools, farm animals, &c., contributed to the farms, and to 'practise mutual-aid and relief' in such a way as to favour those who were receiving a lower income than before, so that all might be enabled at least to maintain their previous incomes. In villages where there were big differences of income between members, the wealthier and poorer households should, it was recommended, be included in two separate co-operatives. In farms consisting of several villages, the peasants of villages that had formerly been wealthier should be allowed higher incomes and higher bonuses. The revised draft Agricultural Programme, brought out in 1957, set as one of its aims to ensure that by 1962 the average income of co-operative members had caught up with the present income of the upper-middle peasant.

Another result of the earlier difficulties was that it was made

[1] In a report on 21 Feb. 1957 (BBC, Econ. Suppl. No. 255, 28 Feb. 1957).

more difficult for well-to-do middle peasants to withdraw. This should only be allowed as an exception, and then only in the case of the small number who insisted even after being subjected to criticism. It seems likely that from this time the pressure brought to bear on peasants wishing to withdraw became almost irresistible.

In December 1957 the Government made a determined effort to absorb the final 4 per cent., mainly middle and richer peasants, still outside the co-operative farms. These had mostly, as the Government themselves admitted, obtained a higher income working their own land independently than the average co-operative had done.[1] Under a new directive on individual peasants, local People's Councils were empowered to authorize co-operatives to assume supervision of the production plans, tax payments, and sales of such people. The co-operatives were also to undertake the 'education' of the independent peasants, so as to raise their political consciousness (or, in plain English, to make them recognize their duty to join the co-operatives). It was thus evidently now only a matter of time before the entire peasant population was absorbed in the co-operative farms.

As the campaign proceeded, more and more of the peasant households enlisted joined existing co-operatives, and this proportion rose as the movement approached its goal. While the average number of peasant households in a producer co-operative was at one time twenty-six, by the end of 1956 there was an average of 200 households in the advanced co-operatives. In most areas the co-operative farm coincided with the former village, though in the 'hilly areas' there might be farms covering several villages. A directive of September 1956 had stated that co-operatives should be about 300 house-holds in the plains (this would normally cover several villages), 200 in the 'hilly areas', and 100 in mountainous areas. In a speech made on 21 February 1957, however, Teng Tze-hui announced that there were then about 760,000 co-operatives, which would mean that there was an average of about 160 families, or perhaps a total population of about 600–700, in each farm. During 1957 the authorities seem to have decided

[1] An article in the *People's Daily* in Oct. 1957 admitted that the unit-area production of the well-to-do middle peasants was often about 20–30 per cent. higher than that of newly established co-operatives.

that the farms should become still smaller. It was said that in very large farms the administration became unwieldy and undemocratic, and the members 'lost enthusiasm'. Thus, though there should normally continue to be one co-operative per village, when this had more than 100 households there might be more than one farm in each village. In some cases there might be one large co-operative, having under it several sub-co-operatives or large production brigades, acting as autonomous units, and having their own profit-and-loss accounts. This was evidently intended to make more apparent to each peasant his own financial stake in increased production efforts.

The structure and organization of the farms were defined in the Draft Model Regulations for Agricultural Producers' Co-operatives published on 1 July 1956,[1] and in subsequent CCP directives of September 1956 and September 1957. The farms were supposed to be run on the system of 'democratic management'. The basic organ was the general meeting, consisting of all members of the farm, meeting at least twice a year. This elected the director, deputy director, and members of the management committee, and the chairman and members of the control committee, adopted the constitution of the farm, examined and approved the production plan, the budget, and plans for the distribution of income submitted by the management committee. It was in theory the final arbiter on all points. If necessary some matters might be dealt with by representative meetings, consisting of elected representatives making up not less than one-tenth of the total membership of the farm.

The director and deputy director were concurrently chairman and vice-chairman of the management committee, and one of them had to be a woman. The management committee, having about 9–19 members, administered the affairs of the co-operative 'in accordance with the constitution of the co-operative and the resolutions of the general meeting'. It might appoint the chiefs of the production brigades and production teams with 'the concurrence of the brigade or team members'. The control committee was supposed to see that the management committee carried out resolutions of the general meeting, investigate accounts, and generally supervise the affairs of the farm.

[1] BBC, Econ. Suppl. No. 234, 27 Sept. 1956.

For agricultural work members were divided into production brigades, sometimes subdivided into production teams. The directive of September 1956 considered that brigades should be of about 20–40 households, and teams of about 7–8. These would normally consist of groups of neighbouring peasants, farming specific areas of land with specially assigned animals and farm tools. Members were normally paid by piece-work according to their own work-quota, but teams which over-fulfilled their quota might get a bonus, whereas those which failed might get a smaller entitlement for each work-day per-formed. Sometimes a contract system might be adopted, under which a task was assigned to a certain team at a certain price, after which the team might handle it in any way it chose. After an individual member had fulfilled his work-day quota for a period, which might be a month, season, or year, he might do what he liked till the next period began.

The farm's capital was obtained mainly from funds, seeds, animals, and other assets set aside each year according to the decisions of the management committee and general meeting. In addition, share funds might be collected from the members when they joined. Contributions of animals, tools, &c., might be reckoned as share funds (alternatively lump-sum payments, or a payment over a number of years, might be made by the farm for these); but fowls, domestic animals, and small farm tools were kept by the individual member. When necessary members might invest more money in the co-operative. The co-operative might also borrow from the People's Banks and the supply and marketing co-operatives.

The income of the farm, less the amounts set aside, was distributed to the members at the end of the year, or sometimes as advance payments, according to the number of work-days worked and bonuses earned. Individual members were allowed to engage in subsidiary occupations at home on condition that this did not interfere with the production of the co-operative. They might also, as on the Russian collectives, have a small plot for their own personal use. This was proportionate to the size of the family, but the share per head was not to be more than 5 per cent. of the average share of land in the farm per head. Since in many areas the share of land per head was probably only about a sixth of an acre, this amount must often have been scarcely enough to give a couple of rows of cabbages. Members were in theory free to withdraw with their share of land, or land of similar quality and acreage.

In practice it is quite clear that the organization was not quite so democratic as this theoretical description might indicate. The chairman, and probably many other of the principal officials elected, were almost certainly always Communist Party nominees, if not Party members. The 'elections' were probably as carefully organized and controlled as are other elections in Communist countries. In addition, strict supervision of the farms was undertaken through the local Communist Party Committees. The effective control seems to have come to rest almost entirely with the management committee, probably dominated by the chairman and a few other politically reliable workers, while the participation of the general meeting became only a formality.

During 1957 the authorities themselves became much concerned over the discontent that the authoritarian structure of the farms was arousing. Meetings were held to publicize the importance of 'truly democratic' management. General meetings and representative meetings were to be called to discuss and examine problems of work organization, production teams, work quotas, and cadres' compensation for administrative work. Cadres should consult with co-operative members, and ask veteran members for suggestions on production plans, technical measures, and work norms, before submitting proposals to the management committee and to representative meetings for decision. Later in the year, during the rectification movement to check 'commandism' by CP members, a CP directive demanded the calling of meetings at which cadres would be criticized by the farm members. There should be small-scale meetings attended by representatives of the masses in the co-operatives to 'find facts', and discover the responsibility for mistakes and shortcomings; the officials concerned should then 'speak themselves white', i.e. confess their faults, at mass meetings. Those who had made mistakes should be warned, and, if their mistakes were serious, action should be taken against them.

District Communist Parties were also to cease simply appointing cadres, and ensure that they were elected according to the constitutions of the farms. Production brigades should become smaller (about twenty households) and should be allowed greater autonomy: they should not have all their work planned for them down to the last detail like a gang of labourers. Details of financial receipts and expenditure, including the supplementary payments to cadres, relief payments (for families in difficulties), loans, &c., were always to be made public. The confusion between the administration of the co-operatives and the local Communist Parties should be eliminated and the 'erroneous tendency of holding too many concomitant jobs by Party, government, and co-operative cadres' was to be avoided. Income was to be distributed six or seven times a year, instead of only once. The proportion of land per head made available for individual cultivation was to be increased to 10 per cent., and members had to be allowed sufficient time to work this. All cadres had themselves to take part in production work some of the time, instead of leading a gilded existence as a ruling class at the expense of the other members. The state targets for production were to be replaced by purchasing targets only, so that farms would be able to make their own annual, five-year, and ten-year plans on the basis of the national plans for agriculture.

It is clear that there were at that time serious 'contradictions within the people' on the co-operative farms. Many of the members had begun to feel that they had been reduced to the status of hired labourers, subject to the commands of the privileged few who, through political orthodoxy or official favour, ruled the farms. The new measures were an attempt to provide a safety valve for such discontent, providing at least the appearance of a greater degree of participation by ordinary members on the running of the farms. Within the next year, however, the situation they were designed to meet was entirely transformed by the emergence of a completely new form of social organization in the countryside.

In June 1958 it was announced that 9,200 co-operatives in Liaoning province had been merged into 1,500 larger ones, having an average membership of nearly 2,000 households. It was said that such larger co-operatives were more efficient in the mobilization of manpower, materials, and financial resources, and were thus better equipped to undertake water-conservancy projects, capital construction work, and other measures for increasing production. In July it was announced that in Peking, Tientsin, and other cities housewives had been setting up crèches, communal kitchens, laundries, and other services, so 'freeing women from household drudgery' and enabling them to go out to work in the factories.

In August the first details were given of the movement to set up communes which had first started in Honan.[1] This movement was rapidly extended to all other provinces. By the end of November 26,000 People's Communes had been set up, covering about 98 per cent. of the farm population. On an average, they were made up out of about thirty co-operatives each and contained a population of about 25,000, though there were fairly big variations in size.

The communes took over all the administrative functions of the *hsiang*, previously the lowest unit of local government. The Hsiang People's Congress became the Commune People's Congress, the Hsiang People's Council became the Commune Administrative Committee, the chairman of the *hsiang* became chairman of the commune, and the secretary of the *hsiang* Communist Party Committee became the secretary of the Commune Communist Party. The new unit took over control of all the agricultural and industrial resources of the area, the administration of the local branches of state ministries and organs of the supply and marketing co-operatives and state shops, and of all the educational facilities in the area. They established a local militia, to which in most cases the entire male population belonged, set up credit committees, which handled the savings of members and acted as a bank within the communes, established old people's homes and public cemeteries, and ran the communal kitchens, dining-rooms, and nurseries which were instituted in the new communities. They became responsible for the collection of agricultural tax and industrial and commercial taxes, and of the profits of the enterprises under their management.

[1] See above, p. 68.

All privately owned plots of land, livestock, trees, and even housing were, as a rule, handed over to the communes. Sometimes a small number of domestic animals and poultry could be retained in private ownership. The shares invested in the co-operatives remained registered under the communes, but no interest was paid.

The communes are normally organized into a number of production brigades, which are themselves divided into production teams. There usually seem to be a score or so brigades in each farm, each covering all fields of economic activity. Each brigade has its own profit-and-loss account which is, however, absorbed by that of the commune as a whole. The production team is the basic unit of labour organization and, sometimes at least, specializes in different branches of the farm's activities. A general meeting of members of the teams elects a team leader and a certain number of deputy leaders, forming a committee to lead its work. Members of each brigade elect deputies to the Congress of the commune; these deputies elect a brigade leader, a deputy leader, a management committee, and a supervisory committee, as in the old co-operatives, to which the brigade may perhaps correspond. The communes seem, however, to have been run partly on an experimental basis at first and the organization was not always the same in different provinces. In any case it was claimed that as a result of the establishment of larger units, the work of fertilizing and irrigation had been improved and it had been made possible to provide better facilities for implement repair, for the manufacture of ball-bearings for agricultural tools, and for producing fertilizer and other requirements.

Roughly half the total distribution to members is made by monthly wage-payments, while the rest takes the form of the free supply of meals, clothing, housing, and sometimes other services, such as weddings, hair-cutting, cinemas, and so on. The former work-point system, under which payment was made according to the number of notional work-days contributed to the communal work of the co-operative, was abandoned in favour of a system of basic wages, assessed according to 'labour performance and work attitudes', plus monthly and seasonal awards. This change was said to help bridge the gap between proletariat and peasant, but was no doubt largely a reflection of the fact that any element of free choice was eliminated under the new system, so that each member was, like a labourer, obliged to work a full working week on the task allotted to him.

The communes were not to be entirely independent economically. They were to formulate plans for production, capital construction, sales of their products, circulation of commodities, and purchases of machinery and equipment, which were to be submitted to the state planning organizations for 'examination, endorsement, and balancing'. In addition, many communes were organized into loose federations of communes which perhaps correspond roughly to counties: these may represent the next stage in the development of 'communal ownership'.

The communes were called on to 'organize their activities with high militancy' and so 'improve their productive efficiency and labour discipline'. One of the advantages of the system was said to be that members had become disciplined by the large-scale collective labour system and as a result 'tremendous changes had taken place in their moral views, state of consciousness and living habits'. Although communes were said to have been established as a result of spontaneous action on the part of the peasants, one of the essential conditions of their successful formation was said to be that all should follow 'the correct principles and policies of the CCP central and provincial committees'.

Already towards the end of 1958, however, the communes seem to have run into some difficulties, many of them the same as had previously beset the co-operatives. There were repeated calls for thorough rectification, to ensure that there was no commandism on the part of local cadres, some of whom believed that since the formation of the People's Communes 'they could do anything they wanted and have anything they liked, and that any talk about the mass line was no longer necessary'; there were demands that a system of genuine democratic management should be maintained; commune members should not be overworked and should be assured of a minimum time for sleep and recreation; an article published by Li Hsien-nien in *Red Flag*, the principal ideological journal of the régime, emphasized the need to 'avoid dampening the enthusiasm of the original co-operatives and brigades in running their own economy'; communes were called on to make proper allowances for the difference in productive capacity of different families and for the previous living standards of different co-operatives when arranging distribution; there were demands that the newly established free supply system should not deprive commune members of all freedom of choice in food and clothing. It appears likely, therefore, that as earlier in the co-operatives many ordinary commune members were becoming increasingly restless at the restrictions on their freedom and independence which had manifested themselves in the communes and that, in particular, those who had previously been best off were not always happy at finding their standard of living reduced to that of the average member.

Towards the end of the year some steps seem to have been taken to remedy these strains. Cadres were ordered to ensure, in carrying out distribution, that the income of 90 per cent. of the members should exceed their previous income, and that none should have less than they got before. The Hupeh CCP recommended that supplementary payments should be made to those members who had previously been better off, or who provided more in manpower to production. Cadres were to take part in productive work, and to ensure that they were fully in touch with the sentiments of the masses. Members were to be 'educated to love the communes'. Finally, on 19 December 1958, the Central Committee of the CCP issued a new directive which, without slowing down the pace of the projected transition from 'communal ownership' (i.e. ownership and management by the communes with distribution according to its own requirements) to 'ownership by the whole people' (i.e. ownership and management by the state with reward according to the national economic requirements),[1] seemed designed to check precipitate or authoritarian action by over-enthusiastic local cadres, and to ensure that nothing should be done to antagonize other members unnecessarily. 'The scope of the free supply system' should not be 'too wide'; big differences in wage-rates might still be permitted; members could keep small

[1] The directive reaffirmed that the commune was to remain the basic unit of organization in the fully Communist society (*NCNA*, Suppl. No. 18, 19 Dec. 1958).

farm tools, trees, small animals, and poultry, and could engage in side occupations in their spare time; they should be assured of their right to private property, including houses and bank deposits; and democratic practices had to be faithfully adhered to.

During the early part of 1959, all over the country inspection teams were sent out to supervise the organization of the communes. There is no doubt that the primary aim of this inspection was to ensure that local cadres were correctly applying the resolution of 19 December, that attempts to push the communes too fast were halted, that 'commandism' was overcome, that commune members were reassured over their property rights, that they were not grossly overworked and that they should thus, so far as possible, be reconciled to the new system. There were warnings against 'petty trends towards egalitarianism'. Wages were to be graded into six or eight scales (in addition to the free supply). The militia system was not 'to infringe on the democratic life of the commune', a clear indication that the system had been used by some cadres to organize the communes' activities on military lines. At the same time there was to be more careful planning of production and a more realistic allocation of resources. The communes should concentrate principally on subsidiary production for agricultural purposes, tool-repair, fertilizer production, &c., rather than seeking to make themselves independent of exchanges with the factories of the cities.

Greater independence was given to the individual production brigades within the commune. These seem to correspond roughly to the old co-operative farms. They were made once again independent accounting units, contributing to the economy of the commune as a whole, but making an independent distribution according to their own successes in production. Payment in kind was again reduced. Later there was further decentralization. 'Production teams', of about 60–80 members, became the basic working unit. Finally increasing prominence was given to 'work squads', containing only a handful of workers.

The communes nevertheless seem destined to remain the basic administrative unit in the countryside over the next few years. Their functional value has been shown, both in industry and agriculture, to be increasingly questionable, but they are no doubt still valued for their ideological significance, and especially for their appeal to other underdeveloped countries.

By 1 January 1959 about 99 per cent. of the peasants had become members of communes, having an average membership of just under 5,000 households. In addition, there were already at the beginning of 1958 about 700 state farms with 9,500 tractors, having a total cultivated area of about 1 million hectares, employing 420,000 workers and producing over 2 million tons of grain (more than 1 per cent. of the total).

On the whole it is likely that the authorities are well pleased with their success in carrying through, with so little difficulty, what is perhaps the most sweeping and far-reaching measure of social transformation the world has seen, in which the way of living of about a fifth of the earth's population has been radically changed. On ideological grounds alone some form of collectivization of agriculture was inevitable under a Communist Government in China. The process was probably hastened, however, by the Government's belief in the technical advantages of larger units in improving agricultural production, which, it was probably hoped, would more than compensate for any loss of output through reduced enthusiasm among the peasants. Certainly the Government claim that the output and income of most peasants was increased after their absorption into co-operative farms, but there is no evidence that the two facts represent cause and effect. The Government itself admit that many of the upper-middle peasants who remained outside the co-operatives gained higher outputs than those within the farms (though they may have had marginally better land).

On the other hand organization into co-operatives, and, still more, of communes, no doubt facilitated work on irrigation and other forms of capital development. Since today no peasants are apparently allowed to continue to maintain an independent existence, there will no longer be any opportunity to make a true comparison of the productivity obtainable under the two systems; in any case the Chinese leaders are no doubt too far committed by their political religion to allow the possibility of more than one answer to the question.

A second advantage of collectivization in the eyes of the authorities was probably that it made easier the collection of taxation and compulsory deliveries, and made hoarding and speculation more difficult. On their own admission, however, these problems have by no means been eliminated. There were a good many reports of false declarations of output and of illegal retentions of grain for personal consumption by the co-operatives. One of the reasons for the strict supervision exercised over the farms through the agency of trusted officials and the local Communist Party Committees was probably the need to secure the maximum possible control over the produce of the farms. An equally strict control will no doubt be maintained over the militantly organized communes.

Considering the speed and relentlessness with which it was carried out, the programme of collectivization appears, so far as it is possible to judge from outside, to have aroused—anyway until the process was completed—remarkably little active unrest among the peasants, though it is clear that since then there has been at the very least considerable discontent.

There seem to have been several reasons why the Chinese avoided the calamitous effects brought about by the collectivization drive in the Soviet Union. First, they were able to profit by the experience gained by the Russians; thus they were careful to avoid both the violence with which the campaign against the kulak was waged, and the suddenness and unexpectedness of the lightning campaign for wholesale collectivization, in Russia. The Chinese, though destroying the landlord class, were careful in formulating the provisions of the Land Reform Law not to alienate the richer peasant, and seem to have succeeded in integrating him into the new agricultural economy without at the same time forfeiting support from the poorer and landless peasants. At the same time, in introducing their programme of collectivization, they moved by gradual steps, starting comparatively mildly, with the establishment of the mutual-aid teams, which probably seemed harmless enough or even advantageous to many peasants, and only slowly worked their way towards the more advanced forms of collectivization. At each step, therefore, the peasant may have hoped that the current stage was going to last longer than in fact occurred.

But the Government did not conceal the fact that their final intention was the 'socialization of the countryside' and thus the final moves never aroused the violent and impassioned upsurge of feeling that would have occurred if they had been made suddenly and without forewarning.

Secondly, although the peasant can scarcely have welcomed the prospect of having the advantages of private ownership taken away from him almost as soon as his rights had been affirmed in the Land Reform Law, some may well themselves have recognized the purely material advantages that might be won by working the land in larger units, and the gains which could therefore be had from a greater degree of co-operation among themselves. Each of them realized how precarious and inadequate was the living that he could gain from his own plot however hard he worked, and may have been dazzled by the mirage set before him of unparalleled prosperity through collectivization. Powerful inducements were laid before those entering the co-operatives in the form of better credit terms, better implements, and better marketing facilities. Finally, there was certainly very strong moral pressure laid upon each individual peasant by local officials and Communist Party members in his own area, as well as through the intensive propaganda machine in the hands of the Government. By such means the peasant may have been finally induced to make the best of the inevitable, and to resign himself to the loss of his independence and of his so recently established proprietory rights. And once absorbed into the co-operative he probably saw no great difference in the merging of this into a still larger unit. How far such a submissive attitude will persist must depend on the success of the Government in improving living conditions in the countryside, in restraining the authoritarian attitude of local cadres, and in allowing the peasant at least the appearance of a greater say in the way the affairs of the commune are run.

XIV

THE DEVELOPMENT
OF AGRICULTURAL PRODUCTION

AGRICULTURE occupies a place of key importance in the Chinese economy. It is vital, not only to maintain and increase the available food supply for the rapidly growing population, but also because Chinese imports of capital equipment for their industrialization programme, whether obtained from the Soviet Union or from the West, must be paid for principally by exports of agricultural goods. The various trade agreements ana protocols with the Soviet Union, under which Chinese imports of capital equipment have been made, have provided for the supply by China in return of mainly agricultural goods. And China's exports to the West, both now and before the war, have consisted almost entirely of the produce of the countryside. Within China, because of the expansion of industry, cash crops, forestry, and animal husbandry, agriculture is faced, according to the Chinese authorities, with the responsibility of supplying some 200 million people, who cannot provide for all their own needs, with at least some quantity of grain.[1] This number will probably increase with the growth of the population and of industry. Thus, although at first the Government gave considerably less attention to the expansion of agricultural production than to their plans for industrial production, they have recently come to recognize that the vigorous development of the country's agricultural resources is vital to the future growth of the economy as a whole.

Grain production in 1949, when the Government came to power, was about 113 million tons, compared with the previous total of about 150 million. This was the result partly of the disruption caused in many areas in that year by the civil war, and partly of serious flood damage. Even in 1950 and 1951 total production of food grains was only 132 and 146 million

[1] Of this number half are said to live in the towns and half in the country producing economic crops or engaged in subsidiary occupations.

tons respectively. The figure in the first year was affected by further floods, and in both years by a considerable increase in the area planted to cotton. In both years, too, production may well have been affected by the land-reform campaign. In the early years of the régime the Government's attention in the field of agriculture was, in fact, principally dominated by the question of land reform. Although there were frequent exhortations to increase production, no very specific measures were taken to bring this about, other than the general rehabilitation of the economy, the restoration of law and order in the countryside, and the provision of capital to the peasant through local credit co-operatives.

There was, however, a considerable drive to increase cotton production. This was to make China independent of foreign supplies of cotton, and to ensure that the cotton mills should be able to fulfil the Government's aim of maintaining an ample flow of consumer goods on to the market. The increase was obtained largely by increasing the price paid for cotton by the state and co-operative purchasing organizations, so raising the profitability of cotton production in relation to grain production: this has been the method the Government has used to bring about variations in the production of different crops from the beginning. The campaign was so successful that production of cotton was increased to about 1,300,000 metric tons, or 50 per cent. higher than the highest pre-war, by 1952. An alteration in the price ratio in 1953 brought a slight reduction in output, but production has since risen to about 1,640,000 tons in 1957, and a figure of 3·35 million tons claimed for 1958. As a result, and by dint of stringent cloth rationing, China is now almost self-sufficient in cotton.

The authorities also began soon after their assumption of power to tackle the question of the erosion of the soil which, despite intensive use of natural manures had, as a result of the denudation of the land of its original covering of timber,[1] become extremely serious in parts of North and North West China. Shelter belts were planted to protect the friable loess soil from the effects of the winds blowing down from the Mongolian

[1] This has mainly been taken for firewood—there are many large areas of the North China plains, originally covered in forest, where, though there are a few isolated trees, a wood, even a small one, is a rare sight.

deserts. All over the area the planting of trees was put in hand to hold down the powdery top soil. Ambitious plans for planting were set out in the two Five-Year Plans and in the Twelve-Year Plan for Agriculture announced in January 1956. It is claimed that during the first Five-Year Plan 10 million hectares were afforested, bringing the total forest area to 50 million. There are plans for the afforestation of a further 50 million hectares during the next ten years, raising the proportion of forest from 10 to 20 per cent. of the total land area. It was said during the Great Leap Forward of 1958 that over 20 million hectares of this area had already been planted in that year. There is no indication, however, what proportion of the saplings planted in fact survive (the Ministry of Afforestation periodically demands that greater attention should be paid to this problem), or of what density of planting is necessary to constitute 'afforestation'; and it is possible that many of the grandiose claims that are made in this field may be misleading.

In 1952 output of grain was said to have exceeded the highest pre-war figure for the first time, and production of about 164 million tons was claimed.[1] This figure was barely exceeded the next year, although the Plan had originally provided for an increase of 9 per cent. (later reduced to 6 per cent.): the actual increase was less than 1 per cent. In 1954 the Yangtze and Huai River floods were described as 'almost without parallel' in a hundred years. It was claimed that the main cities were protected, and that the damage was kept within bounds, but it was admitted that about one-tenth of the farm land of the country, or over 10 million hectares, was flooded. In these circumstances production of 169 million tons in 1954 was probably considered a fair performance. Nevertheless, it may have been partly as a result of the difficulty which the

[1] Some Western commentators have suggested that Chinese figures for agricultural production are expressed in terms of the 'biological yield', an estimate made before the harvest which tends to inflate the figure given. This system was formerly used in the Soviet Union and the Eastern European countries, but has now been abandoned by them. There appears to be no evidence on what system is used by the Chinese Government. The fact that estimates of production are sometimes revised downwards after the end of the year might perhaps indicate that the final figures are based on the crop actually harvested. Even if this is the case, however, crop reports by local officials, anxious to maximize their own achievements, may well tend to give an inflated picture, particularly of the amounts of grain retained by local peasants.

Government seems to have had in increasing grain production, and particularly deliveries, during this period, despite substantial increases in the area in cultivation and the expenditure of considerable sums on the import of fertilizers, that the Government decided during 1955 to embark on their programme of collectivization.

Provision for the development of agriculture was made in the Five-Year Plan published in 1955. Agricultural production was planned to increase by about 23 per cent. over the five-year period, or an average of 4·3 per cent. a year, a very high target. The total allocation for capital construction in agriculture, forestry, and water conservancy in the Plan was 3·62 billion yuan, or 7·6 per cent. of the total, compared with 24·85 billion yuan, or 58·2 per cent. of the total, on industry. In fact, during the Plan, agricultural investment reached 3·81 billion yuan, about the same proportion of the total actually invested in industry. About 10 billion yuan was also to be invested by the peasants themselves, i.e. on purchases of fertilizers, tools, &c. This was said in the event to have reached 12 billion yuan. During 1953–5 capital investment in agriculture by the Government amounted to less than 3 per cent. of total capital investment during that period, compared with over 50 per cent. for government investment in industry. Total government expenditure on agriculture was, of course, far bigger. The Minister of Agriculture announced in November 1957 that the Government had spent about 12,800 million yuan (£1,800 million at the official rate of exchange) on agriculture during the period of the Plan; even this is little more in monetary terms than the current rate of expenditure by the British Government on the support of agriculture in the United Kingdom; and in real terms the volume of assistance is probably lower.

In trying to justify this disproportion between capital expenditure on industry and agriculture the Government have argued that the ratio between industrial and agricultural investments was appropriate in the light of present conditions of agricultural production in China. Since mechanization of agriculture could not yet be realized because of the backward condition of industry, and its resultant inability to produce farming machinery in anything like sufficient quantities, the development of agriculture must for the moment rely mainly on the introduction of mutual aid and co-operation, better employment of labour, and fuller utilization of land for any increases which were to be obtained.

The real reasons, however, are undoubtedly different. In the first place, for all underdeveloped countries the development of a powerful industrial potential is more immediately attractive to national ambitions than the apparently drab and unexciting task of increasing agricultural output. And in China there is a second factor of almost equal importance. This is the over-population of the country, and the consequent abundance of labour for agricultural purposes. Agriculture is already highly intensive in labour and fairly intensive in capital. Where labour is cheap and plentiful, there is no urgent need of machinery, which could only increase the over-population problem. The need for intensive mechanization will arise only when, if ever, a sufficient labour force has been drawn off into industry to reduce the surplus of labour in the countryside. Meanwhile the scarce capital resources of the country are, in Communist eyes, better employed in building up the foundations of heavy industry.

One of the methods used by the Government to raise agricultural production during the Plan was an increase in the total area of cultivated land. Land is normally reclaimed, as in Russia, by state farms. This is probably the principal reason for the big increase in the total area cultivated by the state farms in the course of the Plan. The area brought into cultivation has been principally in remote regions such as north Manchuria, Sinkiang, and Hainan, and there have been large-scale movements of population from hitherto over-populated regions, for example Shantung, Hopei, and Honan, to the newly worked regions. In 1956, 260,000 people were moved from these three provinces to Heilungkiang Province alone. Much of the land may be ground that was hitherto not thought worth cultivating, so that its fertility may not be very high, at least without substantial irrigation. The Government claim, however, that 30–35 million hectares, equal to about a third of the present cultivated area of China (about 100 million hectares), are worth reclaiming. About 4 million hectares were said to have been reclaimed between 1953 and 1956. This is equal to just over half of the total cultivated area of Britain, and compares with about 36 million hectares reclaimed during the Russian virgin-lands programme. It is hoped to reclaim a further 5 million hectares by the end of the second Five-Year Plan.

Related to this programme there has been an intensive effort to develop the so-called 'hilly regions' (which consist largely of mountains). These represent about two-thirds of the total area of China, but contain only about one-third of the cultivated land. A large proportion of the cadres and other urban workers who were packed off to the countryside during 1957 were to go to these regions. A programme proposed by the Rural Work Department of the CCP, in November of 1957, called for the completion of a comprehensive programme to develop the hilly areas, including the development of communications, small industries, and the handicraft industry, and a programme for water and soil conservation. Special attention was to be paid to the establishment of processing, mining, and other small-scale industries. The programme was described by Chu Teh as 'one of the chief tasks of the second Five-Year Plan'.

Within the total cultivated area there has been an effort to increase the area that is irrigated. During the first Five-Year Plan 14 million hectares are said to have been added to the previous total, three times the target of the Plan. As a result the total area was increased to over 34 million hectares, nearly a third of the total cultivated area. But the main effort in this field was launched at the beginning of the second Five-Year Plan. In the winter of 1957–8 a further 33 million hectares was said to have been added to the irrigated area, and by the end of 1960 it was claimed that 60 per cent. of the cultivated area had been irrigated. Most of this work was done by the peasants themselves under the direction of the commune or *hsiang*, and consisted of the construction of ditches, storage pools, pumps, devices for raising water, and similar works. Sometimes it included the construction of tiny hydro-electric power stations with a capacity of not more than 40 or 50 kilowatts which could nevertheless be used for pumping, and to run local flour mills, plants for cotton ginning and oil pressing, and similar purposes. (Publicity was devoted to one station built in five days and having a capacity of 7 kilowatts.)

Various other campaigns were instituted to improve agricultural productivity as a whole. There was a big effort to improve the numbers and the handling of draught animals. The total number of large domestic animals was said to have increased from 60 million in 1949 to about 88 million in 1956, though the increase had been only very slight between June 1954 and June 1956. On the other hand, of this number the total number of draught animals had decreased since 1949. In December 1955 and January 1956 directives were issued strictly forbidding the slaughter of draught animals. It is possible, therefore, that there occurred in China, on a restricted scale, the same phenomenon of the slaughter of animals at the time of collectivization as took place in Russia. Peasants may well have considered that the capital value of the animals to themselves would only be slight within the co-operatives, and that they might as well try to obtain the best price they could for the carcasses (which would almost certainly be better than the compensation paid by the co-operatives) while the going was good. A government directive of March 1957 therefore demanded that better prices should be given for animals on entry into the co-operatives, recommended that these animals should be given to individual peasants, usually the original owners, to look after separately on entry (the peasant would thus be allowed at least the illusion of continued ownership), and called for higher prices for meat and hides to encourage breeding, and better plans within the farms for growing suitable fodder. The inclusion of a passage on the better care of draught animals was one of the few changes made in the revised version of the draft Twelve-Year Plan for Agriculture issued in October 1957. As a result, by the end of 1958 the number of cattle, horses, mules, and donkeys was said to have risen to over 90 million; not a large total among a peasant population of 500 million.

There was also a campaign to increase the number of pigs kept. These were needed not only for meat—there had been severe shortages of pork in many parts of China—but also to fertilize the ground. Total numbers were said to have declined from 100 million in June 1954 to 84 million in June 1956; this

again may have been in part an effect of the co-operative movement, though it was probably due more to inadequate procurement prices. The Government admitted that prices had been
too low, and said that increased procurement of grain had
caused a shortage of fodder. A directive early in 1957 called for
a rapid increase in the number of pigs. Prices were raised by
14 per cent., and the Government decreed that pigs might be
kept by individual peasants as well as by the co-operative as a
whole. Peasants could acquire pork coupons as part payment
for their pigs. By the end of 1959 there were said to be about
180 million pigs. At the end of 1958, it was said, there were
about 125 million sheep and goats, nearly double the number
in 1952.

Big efforts have been made to increase the use of chemical
fertilizers. Domestic production, which was running at about
100,000 tons a year in 1957, was scheduled to increase to 15 or
20 million tons a year by 1962. Meanwhile there have been
urgent attempts to persuade the Chinese peasant to collect and
use greater quantities of farm-yard manure and other refuse.
An intensive campaign has been waged to induce him to plough
deeper and plant closer. At the same time he has been called
on to adopt more modern implements and to improve those he
has. Many of the tools used by Chinese peasants today are little
if any different from those employed two thousand years ago.
Members of co-operatives were encouraged to adopt new and
more efficient seed drills, hoes, water-lifting equipment, and
sprayers; insecticide sprayers and rice-transplanting machines
were publicized; great efforts were made to persuade the
peasant to make use of the double-shared ploughs which for
long lay rusting in the fields because he did not understand
them or considered them unsuitable; and every farm was called
on to manufacture its own ball-bearings and insert them in all
tools having moving parts.

An effort was made during 1957 to boost the production of
economic and subsidiary crops, which tended to be depressed
as a result of the pressure for the maximum procurement of the
main crops. There was to be greater production of oil-bearing
plants, especially castor-beans, sunflowers, tung and tea-plants,
which could be grown in infertile soil. Peasants were also to be

given plenty of time for their subsidiary occupations. Efforts were to be made to ensure that every corner of land, including the raised borders between fields, the edges of railway embankments, the banks of rivers and canals, and unused courtyards should be used. The area where double-cropping was practised was to be increased. This was to be extended from the extreme south, where it already prevailed, to cover the whole of the Yangtze valley; while during the second Five-Year Plan about half the paddy-land of central China was to be switched to double-cropping. At the same time in many areas dry-field cultivation was to be changed to wet-field. Efforts were made to develop the production of rubber, hemp, coffee, and coconuts in the tropical areas of Kwangtung and Hainan.

The Chinese authorities were fortunate in attaining, despite not too favourable weather conditions, a fairly high level of agricultural production in the years in which the collectivization programme was being suddenly rushed to its conclusion. Serious set-backs in production in these years might have had a disastrous effect on the collectivization programme, and possibly even on the political stability of the country as a whole. It is impossible to say whether the better results were in any way the result of the collectivization programme. Procurement was probably more efficient. It is also possible that collective methods improved the technical standards of the less efficient farmers, though there must almost certainly have been a corresponding loss through decline in enthusiasm. The continued increase in production was probably due far more to the first effects of the use of improved strains, increased application of fertilizers, better irrigation, and the reclamation of previously uncultivated land.

In fact grain production (including soya beans) in 1955 was claimed as 184 million tons, and in 1956, despite the worst calamities since 1949, affecting over 15 million hectares, as 193 million, bringing the level to over 25 per cent. above the highest pre-war figure (but it should be remembered that during the same time the Chinese population had probably increased by more than this, perhaps by as much as 30 per cent.). Production of cotton, however, partly as a result of excessive concentration on grain production and partly because of the adverse weather conditions, fell in 1956 to 1,442,000 tons, 5 per cent. below the 1955 figure.

At the end of 1957 it was announced that the total Five-Year Plan targets for agriculture had been over-fulfilled by 1·4 per cent. Total production (of agriculture and subsidiary occupations) in 1957 had been about 3·5 per cent. above the 1956 figure. Food-grain production had reached 185 million tons, excluding soya-bean production, which the previous year had amounted to about 10 million tons. Production of grain and beans together was thus probably little bigger than in 1956. Production of cotton was estimated at about 1,640,000 tons, about 14 per cent. above the 1956 crop (which had been bad).

It is fairly clear that towards the end of the first Five-Year Plan, probably as a result of the inflationary pressures that were making themselves felt at this time, the Chinese Government decided to lay increasing emphasis on the development of agriculture. Several of the Communist leaders said that the development of agriculture was lagging behind that of industry, and that this situation must be remedied.[1] It was announced that during the second Plan the proportion of total investment funds to be spent on agriculture would be increased to 10 per cent. against 8 per cent. during the first Five-Year Plan. Much of the increase in investment in agriculture was to come from the peasants themselves, however, whose total capital accumulation (only a part of which represents net investment) would be increased by 50 per cent. to 18,000 million yuan. The co-operatives were called on to devote more work-days, perhaps 10 per cent. of the total, to capital construction, i.e. work designed to increase the productive capacity of the farms, and to raise more pigs to improve the soil. The state for its part was to concentrate on investment in essential medium and large-scale water conservancy projects, afforestation, tractor stations, and pumping stations. The production of artificial fertilizers was to be increased and two new tractor plants in Loyang and Tientsin would start production.

In 1958, the year of the Great Leap Forward, the authorities claimed an almost unbelievable increase in the production of

[1] See above, p. 66.

both grain and cotton. The total grain harvest was said to be about 375 million tons, almost exactly double that of the previous year, and production of cotton 3·35 million tons, also just over twice the 1957 total. There were similar claims for other crops. There may well have been a bumper harvest in China in 1958. But the claim to have doubled yields within a single year was one that could not be seriously credited. It must very quickly have been doubted in China itself. Already at the end of the year there were reports of shortages in certain fields, vegetables, flour, and even grain. It is possible that the introduction of the 'free supply system', and the strenuous exertions of the peasants during the winter months, previously a slack season, had brought about some increase in consumption in the countryside. But a harvest on the scale claimed could have provided for almost unlimited consumption in China, as well as huge exports. Every stomach could attest the implausibility of the claims. In the face of this situation, in August 1959 the Government were forced to admit that 'owing to lack of experience', the agricultural statistical organs had 'in most cases made an over-assessment', and the figure of grain production in 1958 was reduced from 375 million to 250 million tons.

At the same time the target figure for 1959 was cut in half, being reduced from 525 to 275 million tons. But weather conditions in 1959 were bad. There were floods in the south in the early part of the summer, while there was drought in Manchuria and, later, in the Yangtze area. There were emergency measures for planting supplementary late-maturing crops. The eating of grain mixed with vegetables, stalks, and roots was encouraged. A State Council directive recommended the collection of wild plants to supplement farm produce. Grain production, claimed to be 270 million tons, was lower than the year before.

The Chinese leaders again had to defend the policy of exporting grain to the Soviet Union. And at the beginning of 1960 there was a new concentration on agricultural problems. The state factories were to supply more machinery, iron and steel, and fertilizers for agricultural purposes. There was another intense irrigation campaign. In the next year, however, natural

conditions were even more unfavourable than the year before.
There was a prolonged drought in the spring, which even the
intensive irrigation work already undertaken could not overcome. Later there were typhoons and floods in Central and
South China. In Manchuria floods overran mines and factories
and virtually stopped production in some of the large cities.
There were reports of famine in some districts. The calamities
were said to have been the worst known for decades. But it is
likely that there were more fundamental reasons for the failure
to achieve satisfactory levels of production.

In January 1956 the Chinese Government published their
draft national programme for agriculture, a Twelve-Year Plan,
to run from 1956 to 1967. This, drawn up by the Political
Bureau of the Central Committee of the CCP, provided a
number of highly ambitious targets for agriculture, covering
the period of three Five-Year Plans. Other targets will be set
in each Five-Year Plan, and in the annual Plans. The draft
programme was submitted for discussion and approved by the
Central Committee of the CCP in April 1956. A revised
programme, whose targets, however, were not significantly
altered, was published by the Central Committee of the CCP
in October 1957. The Plan was finally passed only in April 1960.

Within the twelve-year period production of grain is, under
this Plan, to increase by two to five times, varying in different
regions, and of cotton by nearly three times, largely as a result
of improved yields. Increases in grain yields of 100–170 per cent.
and increases in cotton yields of 80 to nearly 200 per cent.
(bigger increases are hoped for in the north of the country where
yields are now lower than in the south) are to be achieved. To
increase the area of high yielding crops, the area under rice is
to be extended by some 17 million hectares and the area sown
to maize and potatoes is to be increased. To increase the production of natural fertilizer, the number of pigs is to reach an
average of 1½–2 per household by 1962, and 2½–3 by 1967. The
total area of irrigated land and paddy-fields was to increase
from 26 million hectares in 1955 to 60 million hectares in 1967:
though according to official figures this total has already been
surpassed; 100 million *mou* of waste land is to be reclaimed by
the state farms.

Various other measures to increase production are outlined in the Plan, including water-conservancy schemes, the use of improved farm tools, the gradual introduction of mechanization, the use of selected seed, soil improvement, the extension of the area of multiple crops and high yielding crops, improvement of farming methods, reclamation of land, the dissemination of scientific information, and emulation campaigns. The production and use of new-type farm tools are to be encouraged: some 6 million double-shared wheel ploughs are to be put into operation, with a corresponding number of sowers, cultivators, sprayers, harvesters, shellers, and ensilage cutters. The use of fertilizer is to be widely encouraged. Selected cotton seed will be used on a large scale; and selected seed for such major crops as rice, wheat, maize, soya beans, millet, kaoliang, potatoes, sesame, sugar-cane, tobacco, and hemp are to be in general use within seven to twelve years. In addition, the Plan, which covers the whole field of rural life in China, sets ambitious targets for the development of afforestation, communications, health, and for coping with illiteracy, housing, unemployment, and other matters.

An effort is to be made to increase labour productivity. It is considered that in seven years, starting from 1956, every able-bodied male worker in the countryside should be able to put in 250 working days per year, and every able-bodied woman 120 working days a year; this is perhaps intended to increase the amount of labour devoted by peasants in slack periods to irrigation and other 'capital construction' work. Scientific research is to be developed, and large numbers of technical agricultural cadres are to be trained. Credit co-operatives will be set up in almost every *hsiang* to promote rural credit and rural savings. To tackle the vexed problem of 'bridging the gap' between town and country, which so preoccupies Marxist theorists, workers and peasants should 'by means of getting together, visits, correspondence and other means, establish constant contact, encourage each other and exchange experiences'.

The Twelve-Year Plan is clearly intended as a convenient focus for the vast effort which the Government require of China's peasantry. The targets set are highly ambitious, and although the backwardness of Chinese agriculture undoubtedly gives some scope for improved yields, it will not be easy to achieve increases on the scale planned. It is perhaps because they were conscious that the goals they had set themselves might prove to be beyond their attainment that the Government set no specific target for agricultural production during the period of the Plan. The programme may be designed primarily to give rural officials and the rural population throughout the country some idea of the directions in which Chinese agriculture is to be developed over the next twelve years, and to serve as a target and morale-booster, rather than to set any firm aims for the volume, or even the pattern, of production during that time.

In a speech on 21 July 1955 Mao Tse-tung indicated that some mechanization of agriculture would be initiated on a small scale in the period of the first and second Five-Year Plans; but the start of full development would occur only during the third Five-Year Plan of 1963–7, when the use of large-sized agricultural machinery would be increased year by year. Basic completion would have to wait until the fourth or fifth Five-Year Plan, i.e. about 1972 or 1977. More recently, on 1 April 1960, Li Fu-chun said that eventually the full-scale development of the country would require the technical transformation of agriculture. In the first place this will take the form of improvements to existing equipment. Within the next four years there should begin small-scale mechanization of agriculture and water conservancy throughout the nation. Only at the end of ten years would large-scale mechanization be practised. By 1956 there were 14,000 stations for popularizing agricultural technique. It was hoped that at the end of 1960 about 80,000 tractors and 7,000 harvesters would be in use. By the end of 1959 5 per cent. of the farm land was said to be ploughed by tractors, mainly on the state farms.

A programme of mechanization will depend partly on the progress of industrialization. A contrast has been drawn by the Chinese leaders between the different circumstances of China and the Soviet Union, in that in the Soviet Union 'full collectivization' of agriculture was synchronized with the mechanization of agriculture, whereas in China, because of the lack of a developed heavy industry, the co-operativization of agriculture had to precede its mechanization. In fact, however, the important contrast lies in the entirely different nature of the agricultural economies, and the prospects for their development, in the two countries. Because of the abundant and rapidly increasing supply of labour in the Chinese countryside, and the intensive methods of cultivation employed there, it is unlikely that the Chinese Government will give much priority to the development of mechanized forms of agriculture, which would produce social problems out of all proportion to the material advantages gained. In any case the advantages of mechanization for the cultivation of rice, and for holdings divided, as in many parts of China, into narrow terraces, may be limited at present. The resolution on the political report[1] passed at the Congress of the CCP in September 1956 said that

our country will not in the near future be in the position of having an agricultural machinery industry or a chemical fertilizer industry on any large scale. Nor will it be in a position to carry out reclamation of waste land to any great extent, or rapidly to end flood and drought. In these circumstances the best way to increase agricultural production at present is by . . . the initiation of water-conservancy projects; the use of fertilizer; improvement of the soil; the use of improved seeds. . . .

Towards the end of 1958 an important shift in Chinese agricultural policy became discernible. This was shown in the decision, despite the need for every possible increase in agricultural production, to abandon some areas of marginal land and to concentrate resources of labour and fertilizer on the most fertile parts in an effort to secure even higher yields there. In some areas, mainly those which had suffered badly from soil erosion, very drastic reductions in the cultivated area were made. The cultivated area of Shansi, already reduced by a third in 1957–8, was again reduced by a third in 1958–9, while that of Heilungkiang was reduced by a quarter; half the cultivable area of Inner Mongolia was to be abandoned. Some land previously used for grain cultivation was converted to pasture. At the end of 1958 a national soil survey was initiated which would enable decisions to be taken about the reallocation of land for different purposes.

[1] *NCNA*, Suppl. No. 248, 1 Oct. 1956.

There was a call for 'higher output on a smaller quantity of land'. This system was to be introduced gradually to all areas as yields rose. It was said that, in the long run, only one-third of the total cultivable area would be cultivated, one-third would be allowed to lie fallow, and the remainder used for trees and grass. It may be, therefore, that the Government have become convinced, as a result of the problem of erosion, that it might be possible eventually in China, as in other countries, to raise the total annual food production by the introduction of some crop-ley rotation. They may, too, be looking forward to the time when the general rise in living standards in China makes it essential for them to provide an increasing proportion of meat in the diet of the Chinese worker and peasant.

The Chinese undoubtedly hope eventually to achieve sub-stantial increases in production, now that the period of 'social reform' in the countryside is nearly completed. There will undoubtedly be further development of areas so far uncultivated, especially in north Manchuria, but it is unlikely that the total area of productive land can be increased by more than about 20–30 per cent. at most. Yields can certainly be improved further, but the yields now obtained in China are already high in comparison to those achieved in India and most other Asian countries, and the increases that can be achieved are not un-limited. The application of fertilizers, which would certainly make a considerable difference, is limited by the extent of China's domestic capacity (which was about 750,000 tons in 1957 though rapidly increasing), and by the need to reserve the greater part of supplies of foreign exchange for the import of industrial equipment. The development of large-scale irriga-tion is similarly conditioned by the capital expense involved, though much work is being done on small local irrigation works. The authorities may therefore find it more difficult than they suppose to bring about consistent increases in total agricul-tural production on the scale they require.

But the most important factor affecting the achievement of the aims which the Chinese authorities have set for their agricul-ture (even supposing that they do secure the increases in production hoped for) is the present prodigious rate of growth in the Chinese population, which is now rising at the rate of

12–15 million a year, or nearly 100 million every seven years. Unless there is some check on this rate of increase, the authorities are likely to find it as much as they can do merely to feed this ever-growing number, let alone to provide a surplus to finance their industrialization programme. The recent reversal of the official attitude towards the question of birth-control[1] (hitherto anathematized in accordance with Marxist dogma) perhaps indicates that they are now becoming aware that the ambitious tasks which they have set for their agriculture may well be upset by the headlong increase in their own population.

During the last year or two the Chinese Government have become increasingly aware of the urgent need to bring about substantial increases in agricultural production, even to feed their own population, let alone provide substantial exports in exchange for capital goods. As a result there has been a substantial shift of emphasis from industry to agriculture. Despite this effort, agricultural achievements have been more disappointing than ever. It is likely that the Chinese Government will be obliged to continue in the immediate future to devote a greater part of their energies to strengthening agriculture. For this purpose they may be obliged to abandon some of the innovations which ideology has dictated in favour of more traditional methods.

What they really need is to bring about in China something of the same transformation that Japan has accomplished, the simultaneous development of agriculture and industry. Like Japan, China is not rich in natural resources, nor does she have large areas of uncultivated land to develop as the Soviet Union had. She may therefore increasingly follow Japanese methods in agriculture, seeking to bring about substantial increases in existing low yields through a much higher rate of capital investment, especially in fertilizers, the improvement of existing production methods, and a more efficient use of irrigation resources. Until something of this sort is achieved she will not be in a position to realize these industrial aims which remain her principal ambition.

[1] See below, pp. 208–9.

XV

THE CONTROL OF CONSUMPTION

THE policy of planned production contained in the Five-Year Plan increasingly obliged the Chinese Government to adopt a corresponding policy of controlled consumption. The necessity to export large quantities of agricultural produce, the increases in income caused by the investment programme, and the rapid growth in the population gave rise in the course of 1953 and 1954 to an inflationary gap between demand and supply, especially of food and cloth. As a result rationing had to be gradually introduced.

The problem of the procurement of grain from the countryside and of the supply of food in general began to exercise the planners in the first months of the Five-Year Plan. A leading article in the *People's Daily* of 11 April 1953 pointed out that the demand for better quality grain was increasing on all sides, in the towns, the industrial areas, and the countryside. The cultivated area, however, could not be quickly expanded and, with her large population and unmechanized agriculture, China would need many years of effort to remove the discrepancy between the supply of grains and the demand for them. During that period the food problem might well take on the proportion of an emergency.

This forecast was quickly borne out. The situation seems to have deteriorated badly during 1953. In the early part of the year there was severe cold in some parts of the country, accompanied by drought in other areas. Later there were floods in the north, while parts of the south continued to suffer from drought. There were also widespread losses through locusts. The available food supply was still further diminished by the sale of agricultural products to the Soviet Union in return for imports of capital equipment necessary for the industrialization programme. As a result a very severe food crisis arose. The Government claimed that this situation was exploited by some of the peasants, and in particular by speculative grain merchants, who took the opportunity to hold back some of their produce and to extort high prices in private deals.

As a result on 19 November 1953 the Government passed a decree[1] (not published until 28 February 1954) providing for the 'planned' purchase and supply of grain. This made illegal all dealings in grain except through the government agencies, though private merchants were still to be allowed to function as agents of these. In many districts a form of rationing was introduced (though no public announcement about this was made) covering not only grain but, in many areas, flour, cooking-oil, and meat as well. All wholesale trade in food seems to have been taken over by the state, which determined the rations for different categories of the population, fixed the official purchasing prices and maximum retail prices, and handled the trade in food through a network of government marketing centres. In several cities ration books were issued or purchases were made on the basis of census books.

No official information was given about the amount of the ration, which probably varied at different times and in different places according to the available supplies. Reports from those leaving China at about this time indicate that in most places it was probably sufficient, though not lavish. The ration for rice was variously reported as from 20 to 40 lb. a month. It was higher in the towns than in deficiency areas in the country, where the peasants were presumably expected to have acquired at least some grain from other sources. Throughout the country the rice available seems to have been only of a poor-quality, unpolished variety, the best qualities apparently being used for export. The supply of meat and flour seems to have been adequate for the most part, but a severe shortage of cooking fats was reported from some areas. No rationing system was enforced in areas which produced enough for their own consumption.

In 1954 there was an extension of this system to cover cotton. By an order of the State Administrative Council in September of that year[2] 'planned purchase and supply' of cotton and cotton cloth was introduced, and only the state trading companies were to handle transactions in these commodities throughout the country. Private cotton mills were to produce

[1] *NCNA*, 28 Feb. 1954.   [2] Ibid., 14 Sept. 1954.

for state orders, private wholesalers were to wind up their operations, and private retailers to become agents of the state trading companies. Homespun cotton was to be purchased by the state trading companies through the supply and marketing co-operatives, though direct exchange between producers and consumers in their own localities was permitted. Later the planned purchase system was also applied to all oil-bearing crops.

These three crops, grains, cotton, and oil-bearing crops, were the only ones for which the system of 'planned purchase' was employed. Under this system all sales were either to the state or under state control. After payment of taxation the first charge on the peasants was the delivery of their planned quotas, for which a state-determined and modest price is paid through the local marketing co-operatives, varying according to local conditions and the quality of the crop, but in practice probably as low as the purchasing agency could enforce without causing positive hardship to the peasant. The remainder of the crop, not required for personal consumption, could be sold on the state grain markets or on other markets under state control, but nowhere else. On these markets steps could be taken to prevent the growth of speculation, and to ensure against the re-emergence of private grain merchants, if necessary by imposing maximum prices. There was no 'free market' in these products.

For most other crops a different system was used. This was the so-called 'unified procurement programme', covering tea, tobacco, dates, silk, wool, jute, hemp, &c. Originally, there were twenty-three crops involved, but this number was reduced to nine in the spring of 1957 after the introduction of free markets. For these products there were no delivery quotas. They were to be offered for sale in the first place to the state marketing organization, i.e. the supply and marketing co-operatives, or state enterprises and shops, and any amounts not disposed of in this way could then be sold in the free markets.

A system of advance purchase was introduced for some agricultural products. It was laid down that the All-China Federation of Co-operatives might purchase from the peasants, through advance contracts, cotton, peanuts, tea, ramie, jute, hemp, silk cocoons, raw silk, and wool. At the time of the transaction a fixed percentage of the total value was to be paid to the peasants, and the remainder was paid on delivery of the crop. Any contract not fulfilled must be made up for in the next contract entered into. The payments are made in two instalments, one before the spring cultivation and the other before the final application of fertilizer during mid-season cultivation. During 1957 the Ministry of Food planned to make advance payments worth about 635 million yuan (nearly £100 million) for grain and oil crops.

It is clear from Chinese press comment during the early years of rationing that public opinion in China was (probably correctly) attributing the difficulties that had arisen over food supplies to the exports to the Soviet Union, and was demanding either that exports should be reduced or that grain should be imported. The Government tried to defend themselves by saying that, although the supply of grain did not leave much to spare, so long as 'there is a reasonable distribution and appropriate reallocation' there was no need to import grain, and 'a certain amount' could even be exported.[1] But it was admitted that for some time the balance of supply and demand for food would be a fine one; and that the balance would not be secure until agricultural output was considerably increased.

Early in 1955, as a result of the floods of the year before, there was said to have been an abnormal rise in grain sales, both in urban and rural districts, to meet the shortages that had arisen. State grain sales exceeded the normal monthly schedules by a considerable margin. As a result hundreds of thousands of cadres were sent to the countryside, and requests for grain were submitted for 'public discussion and decision'; the object was presumably, by explaining the reasons for the shortage, to attempt to appease the growing dissatisfaction and to moderate the pressure on the market. It was claimed that, as a result of this action, grain sales were quickly restored to normal.

Part of the difficulty seems to have arisen, as in Russia at a similar stage, from hoarding by the peasants, despite the

[1] Chen Yun's report to the National People's Council, 21 July 1955 (BBC, Econ. Suppl. No. 174, 28 July 1955).

Government's efforts to ensure adequate supplies of consumer goods in the countryside. It is clear that the peasants were not attracted by the prices being offered by the Government's monopoly marketing organizations. Officials claimed that the peasants were 'not yet accustomed to the Government's method of buying and selling'. In the early stages of the new system of 'planned buying and selling', therefore, while selling such grain as was unavoidable to the central agencies, they had often been building up private hoards of their own. The Government claimed that there had also been some hoarding of grain by illegal grain merchants, and attempts by rich peasants having surplus grain to hold out for higher prices.

By the summer of 1955 it was officially admitted that there was a serious food shortage. In August 1955, therefore, the Government decided to introduce rationing in all rural areas (as well as in the towns and the districts previously covered), to revise the rationing system for the whole country, and to tighten the system of planned purchase.

The policy adopted provided for further rationing (now officially admitted) of grain and flour, and a revision of the system of planned purchase and supply. Measures to apply rationing in towns 'to ensure fair distribution' to the 100 million or so of the urban population went into effect in all towns, municipalities, and industrial and mining centres before December 1955. The ration in the cities varied according to age, type of work, and grain-eating habits in various parts of the country. Where wheat flour was the staple food, workers on light physical labour got an average each month of about 45 lb. of flour, those on heavy labour 60 lb., and those on particularly heavy work 75 lb.; other workers, including office employees and shop assistants, got an average of about 40 lb., college and middle school students 45 lb., and 'residents in general' 35 lb. Where rice was the staple food the same classification and differentiation were employed, the quantities being about 10 per cent. less than those for wheat flour.

In rural areas households were divided into three categories—those with a grain deficiency, those which were self-sufficient, and those with a grain surplus. Between 80 and 90 per cent. of any surplus was to be bought by the state at 'fair prices', and the remainder was at the farmer's disposal. A peasant in the self-sufficient class would not have to sell any surplus but would also not be able to buy grain. In determining the 'surplus', output of a normal year was taken as the basis, and once fixed, this basis would normally remain unaltered for three years. Classification and re-classification of households was to be decided after discussion with the local population.

The policy aimed at fixing quotas for a three-year period for deliveries, taxation, and prices of grain. This was probably intended to give the peasants some incentive, once the quota was fixed, to increase production as far as possible, so that they might benefit by the better prices obtainable in the grain markets and improve their own consumption. Under the previous system they no doubt often had the feeling that the more they produced the more the Government took away from them. The directive stipulated that in the crop year July 1955–June 1956, 43·25 million tons of grain would be levied in deliveries and taxation, and that this total would remain unaltered for the three-year period.

The 1955 harvest was good. Not only was it possible to make substantial additions to the state reserves of grain, but the grain ration was slightly increased. During the year from November 1955 to November 1956 it was increased by an average of 3–4 catties a month in the cities and small towns. But the natural disasters of 1956 precipitated yet another crisis in the procedure for distribution of grain. The total amount of grain collected by the state was said to have been 2·5 million tons less than the year before—this despite the fact that, according to the Government, there had been an increase in the total production of food grains—while the sales by the state had gone up by 8 million tons. Relief distribution in famine areas was necessary, and the Government had to draw on the state reserves. The situation in cotton, of which the harvest had been 5 per cent. below the previous year, was even more serious.

As a result early in 1957 the grain ration in the towns had to be again reduced by ½–1 catty a month from the increased total. The value of the coupons for cotton cloth had to be 'temporarily' halved from May 1957, and the differential in favour of workers, cadres, and students was abolished, while that in favour of the towns was reduced. The production of cotton cloth by hand-weaving at the farms was forbidden and the sale of cotton cloth made by native methods in the free markets made illegal. There was a general shortage of pork and egg products.

A very strict control of all sales in the state-controlled markets was also introduced. The co-operatives were to make sure of making the proper payments for taxation and deliveries before distributing among their members. Rises in the prices offered for pigs and oil-bearing seeds in September 1956, and a further substantial rise in the price offered for pigs in the spring of the next year, were designed to remedy the shortages in these fields. The consumer had to pay a proportion only of the rise in the price of pigs, but there were nevertheless price rises in pork, and in oil, woollen textiles, salt, and some vegetables. In January 1957 Po I-po had to assure the National People's Congress that exports of food grains, edible oils, and pork would be reduced to meet the country's own needs.

The problem of procurement may have been simplified for the Government by the almost total incorporation of the peasants into co-operatives during 1955–6. The vigilance of Party officials or reliable farm members would make hoarding or evasion by individual farms or members very much more difficult than it had been for individual peasants. The co-operatives were called on to follow a rigid procedure in disposing of their harvest. Each must first set aside enough for minimum human consumption, for seeds, and for fodder according to a set formula; next they must try to fulfil the grain levy (taxation) and grain delivery quotas fixed by the state; only when these targets were met could they distribute the remainder among members for additional consumption or for sale. If an individual peasant over-fulfilled his production quota, 40 per cent. of the excess would go for procurement, that is forced sales to the state, or alternatively (in deficiency areas) the amount of grain to be supplied by the state would be reduced.

During the course of 1956, in order to give a greater incentive to the peasants for production of subsidiary crops, the Government introduced an important modification of their policy for the procurement of these. For some foodstuffs, for example vegetables, fish, egg products, fowls, preserved foods, lotus seeds, &c., the system of unified purchase was abandoned and a free market was established. It was admitted that trade in these products had 'become stagnant', which meant in fact that the prices being offered by marketing co-operatives and state enterprises under the 'unified procurement' system were inadequate to tempt the peasants to grow, or anyway to market, these products. It was now recognized that the 'law of value' still had a place in a socialist society in certain fields, and that the re-establishment of a free market would help to ensure that public demand would, through the agency of the price mechanism, make itself felt more effectively. Markets were established under state supervision, where the specified products could be sold freely, both to the local population and to local merchants at competitive prices. State shops and co-operatives could only deal through 'exchange houses' designed to ensure adequate prices.

It was claimed that an increased flow of goods between town and country was achieved. In some areas, because of 'speculation and hoarding', only the producers themselves and a few registered merchants were allowed to participate. Maximum prices were sometimes fixed. The local authorities in some districts were censured for allowing the markets to get out of hand, prices to rise dangerously, a new class of speculative merchants to re-emerge, and a return to 'petty-bourgeois capitalism' to take place. In general, however, it was admitted that the 'productive enthusiasm' of the peasants had been greatly increased by the move and the Government's propaganda continued to uphold the advantages of the new method. By January 1957 it was said that about a third of all China's agricultural commodities, and one-eighth of the total value of all retail sales, were bought and sold on the free markets.[1]

In practice, as was later revealed, the functions of the markets were somewhat widened. In some of them marketing of goods subject to 'planned purchase', i.e. grain, cotton, and oil-bearing crops, was allowed. Some of the crops still subject to 'unified purchase' went into the free market before the state procurement programme had been fulfilled. Thus, in August 1957, the

[1] *NCNA*, 30 Jan. 1957.

Government issued a new directive. The sale of 'planned-pur-chase' commodities in the free markets was absolutely forbidden. After the state had acquired the planned deliveries of crops, the remainder, not consumed by the peasants themselves, must be sold only to the state purchasing agencies. In certain cases a province or region could open state-supervised grain markets, but no free market in grain should be permitted. The 'unified procurement' commodities (now reduced from 23 to 9), includ-ing tea, silk, wool, dates, &c., would be procured only by state purchasing agencies or the supply and marketing co-operatives, and might not be sold to anyone else. Other products, such as eggs, chickens, ducks, geese, spices, and some Chinese medicines. would continue to be sold in the free market, but if there developed a critical shortage, the provincial People's Commit-tee could declare them unified-purchase commodities, which could then only be sold to state agencies. No government departments or agencies, forces' commissariats or factory canteens, other than those authorized, were allowed to make purchases.

This tightening was part of a general move during the latter half of 1957 to ensure the maximum possible procurement by the state for consumption in the towns, for export, and for the reserves. There was an intensive campaign of 'socialist education', dovetailed into the general 'anti-rightist' movement of the time, to instil recognition of the duty to make the maximum deliveries. Peasants were to be persuaded to put the state first and themselves last. It was said that as a result of these efforts in September and October 46 per cent. more grain entered the state granaries than in the same period in 1956.

One of the reasons for this particularly intensive procurement campaign in 1957 was probably that, during the next winter, the quotas for deliveries for the coming three years were due to be re-negotiated. Thus, while the peasants had every incentive to under-declare their production, the state had a strong interest in maximizing it. In October the Government announced that, while the new quotas were being fixed, the amounts to be levied in taxation, and purchased in deliveries, should not be reduced, while the amount retained by the co-operatives should not be increased. The state-supervised grain markets were to be closed, and all sales would be to the state.

It is fairly clear that, throughout 1956–7, there was very considerable discontent among the peasants at their current standard of living in general, and particularly a feeling of resentment that the inhabitants of the towns were faring better than they were. Chou En-lai told the National People's Congress in June: 'Some people . . . say that our living standards have gone down since the liberation.' Po I-po in a speech made on 23 February said that 'some people were maintaining that the average consumption level of the peasants was lower than before the war'; and in fact Po I-po himself admitted that this was so if the consumption of the landlords and the rich peasants was included, though he claimed that the average consumption of 'most peasants' was higher. The feeling that the people of the towns did better than those in the country, was no doubt an important cause of the 'blind movement of the peasants into the towns'.

As a result, throughout 1957 there was an intensive campaign to convince the peasants that such ideas were unjustified. Elaborate statistics were quoted in support of this contention. The most revealing figures, however, suggested exactly the opposite. In the speech already mentioned, Po I-po stated that the average consumption per person per year in 1956 reached a value of 180 yuan (about £26 at the present rate of exchange) for the workers, against 81 yuan (about £12) for the peasants, 2·22 times as high, though he claimed that this ratio was little different from before the war when the worker's consumption was 2·12 times as high. He admitted that between 1952 and 1956 the consumption level of the workers had increased by 4 per cent., while that of the peasants had gone up by only 3 per cent. The State Statistical Bureau in July announced that the average *per capita* consumption per annum in the urban and rural areas was as follows:

	Urban areas	Rural areas
Food grains	200 kg.	216 kg.
Edible oil	6·4 kg.	1·9 kg.
Meat	7·0 kg.	3·85 kg.
Sugar and candy	3·85 kg.	0·85 kg.
Cloth	20·6 metres	6·6 metres

It was said that the annual average wage of workers was 598 yuan,[1] while that of the peasants was the equivalent of 288; this was explained on the grounds that 'twice as much money was needed to maintain the same standard of living in the towns'. In November 1957 it was admitted that the workers got a bigger ration of pork and edible oil than the peasants, though it was said that efforts should be made to reduce this discrepancy.

The differences in living standards were in fact vigorously defended in an article in the *People's Daily* in April 1957. This said it was natural that the workers should get a higher standard of living because they had to work more intensively than the peasants; they had to work with complex machines; they did not have the seasonal slack periods which the peasants enjoyed; and their work produced more in value than the peasants' work did. The article claimed, in addition, that the workers contributed more to the state financially by their purchases of consumer goods, the profits of which went to the state enterprises, than the peasants did in taxes: it is difficult to believe that this argument can have had much appeal for the envious peasant.

In the autumn of 1958, after the formation of the communes, it was announced that the free markets had 'in the main' ceased to exist. The communes were to follow the state's unified purchasing policy and to sell their products to the state organs in accordance with the state plans. In effect it seems likely that all the produce of the communes which is not sold to the state is taken over by the food agencies within the commune, either to be used in the communal kitchens or for sale in the commune's own food shops. Since payments to the peasants are now either in wages or in 'free supplies' (meals, clothing, &c.), the distribution of harvested grain to the individual farm member has now presumably ceased.

The big harvest that was claimed for both grain and cotton production in 1958 probably to some extent eased the shortages which had earlier faced the Government. Already at the beginning of 1958 the ration of cotton cloth was raised from 5·3 to 6 metres, and at the end of the year it was raised again to

[1] In Nov. 1957 it was announced that the average wage 'for workers and employees' was 636 yuan a year.

8 metres. On the other hand in December 1958 it was announced that, despite the gigantic harvest that had been claimed that summer, in north China the proportion of wheat flour in the basic food ration was to be reduced from 34 to 20 per cent., and cabbages, which had never been rationed at all before, were now to be rationed for the first time. Later there were reports of shortages of grain, vegetables, and oils. After the bad harvest of 1959 such reports became more common. And after the disastrous summer of 1960 it was admitted that there were 'famine conditions' in some areas.

It is clear that the Chinese Government, despite increases in the total level of agricultural production, are still faced with difficulties in providing adequate consumption levels for their rapidly increasing population. Since a very large proportion of the population are children, the situation may get worse before it improves. The natural calamities of 1959 and 1960 have demonstrated how dependent the Government remain on favourable weather conditions for providing adequate food for their mounting population. Some alleviation may be obtained when the country is able to acquire a larger proportion of its export income from industrial exports. But until such developments can be brought about, some form of rationing is likely to continue both in the towns and in the country.

THE PROSPECTS FOR THE FUTURE

XVI

THE FUTURE DEVELOPMENT OF THE CHINESE ECONOMY

THE 'General Line' guiding the development of the Chinese economy, which was proclaimed in 1953 at the beginning of the first Five-Year Plan, provided that within a period of about a further two Plans, i.e. by about 1968, the transitional phase of 'socialist industrialization' would have been virtually completed. By this Communist leaders seem to have meant that by that time they should on the one hand have created the basis of a modern and comprehensive industrial economy in China, and, on the other, have brought about the complete socialization of the country, with all the industrial and commercial resources of the nation in the hands of the state, and the agricultural population completely absorbed in the 'socialist' higher-stage co-operatives or even more advanced forms. This latter aim, the 'socialist transformation' of the country, has now already been almost accomplished. The current aim is to catch up the absolute (as opposed to the *per capita*) production levels of Britain in the principal commodities by 1973.

What, in fact, are the prospects for China as an industrial power? The outputs of the main industrial products which China aimed to achieve at the end of the first and second Five-Year Plans are shown in the table overleaf.

The 1958 output of the principal commodities and those planned for 1962 may be compared with the 1958 rates of output of the United States, the Soviet Union, Great Britain, and India, shown in the table on p. 195.

Three things emerge from these figures. First, the rate of increase in industrial capacity aimed at by the Chinese Government is very high indeed. It is, if anything, even higher than that attained by the Soviet Union at a comparable stage in her history, although since China started from a more backward position and at a time when technology was more advanced, the figures are not strictly comparable. The planned increase is

First and Second Five-Year Plan Targets: Main
Industrial Products

(*million tons*)

Product	Highest pre-Communist output	1952	Target 1957	1957 output	1962 (draft plan)
Coal	61·9	63·5	113·0	124	190–210
Pig-iron	1·8	1·9	4·7	5·86	..
Steel	0·9	1·3	4·1	5·24	10·5–12
Electric power (billion kw.)	5·96	7·26	15·9	19·01	40–43
Crude oil	0·32	0·44	2·0	1·42	5·0–6·0
Metal-cutting machine tools ('000 units)	5·0	13·7	13·0	..	60–65
Cement	2·3	2·8	6·0	6·75	12·5–14·5
Cotton yarn (m. bales)	2·4	2·6	5·0	4·65	8–9
Chemical fertilizer	0·227	0·194	0·57	0·74	3·0–3·2

Sources: First Five-Year Plan; Proposals for Second Five-Year Plan; 1957:
press sources.

almost certainly higher than that being achieved in any other
country in the world today. And, if the results claimed for 1958
are any indication, that rate is at present being exceeded.

Secondly, even in 1962 China will still be unquestionably a
backward country, with figures of industrial production far
lower even than those of the United Kingdom, which has a
population only about one-twelfth the size. The figures will of
course be incomparably lower than those of the United States
and the Soviet Union, while the output per head will show an
even bigger difference. It has been estimated that in 1928, on
the eve of the first Five-Year Plan, Soviet real income per head
was about four times as high as in China in 1952.[1] Even now,
when the first Chinese Plan has been completed, the Chinese
level of production of essential products is not far above the
level of the Soviet Union in 1928.

Thirdly, Chinese production is nevertheless already rather
higher than that of India, the only other underdeveloped

[1] Rostow, *The Prospects for Communist China,* p. 259.

*Output of Principal Commodities: China and Other
Countries Compared*

(*million tons*)

Commodity	China (1958)*	China (1962) (draft plan)	India (1958)	UK (1958)	USSR (1958)	USA (1958)
Coal	270	190–200	46·0	219	360†	389‡
Iron ore	..	..	5·8	14·8	88·8	107·9
Crude steel	11	10·5–12	1·7‡	20·0	55·0	102·0‡
Electric power (billion kwh.)	27·5	40–43	12·0	98·0	234·0	720·0
Oil	2·2	5·0–6·0	—	—	113·0	354·0‡

*Provisional figures. †Including lignite. ‡1957.

Sources: *Proposals for Second Five-Year Plan;* UN, *Statistical Yearbook* and *Monhtly Bulletin of Statistics.*

country of comparable size, and by 1962 the disparity will probably be greater. The Indian second Five-Year Plan provides for the following targets for production of the principal commodities in 1960–1, which may be compared with the Chinese 1962 goals.

Indian and Chinese Production Targets

(*million tons*)

	India (1960–1) (Plan)	China (1962) (draft plan)
Food grains	75·0	245
Coal	60·0	190–210
Steel	4·3*	10·5–12
Electric power (b. kwh.)	22·0	40–43
Oil	..	5–6

* Rolled Steel.

Sources: *India, Planning Commission, Second Five-Year Plan* (Delhi, 1956), p. 336; China, *Proposals for Second Five-Year Plan.*

Of these three conclusions the last is potentially the most important. There are many backward countries in the world in a similar position to India and China, attempting to develop a modern industrial economy within the shortest possible space of time. If they come to believe that the speed of development in China has, over a period, been faster than that achieved elsewhere under different systems of government, they may tend to draw ideological conclusions from the fact, and be tempted to experiment with methods similar to those which have proved successful in China, even if this involves a sacrifice of political freedom for their peoples.

Can the Chinese Government be expected to achieve the industrial goals which they have set themselves? The first condition for the accomplishment of these aims is the maintenance of an adequate level of industrial investment, especially in the basic industries. The Government have engaged in a very high volume of investment in the course of the first Five-Year Plan. The total sum spent on capital construction during the five years is said to have reached 49 billion yuan, or over £7,000 million, 13 per cent. more than originally planned. On the basis of figures given by Po I-po at the CCP Congress, it would appear that investment by the state equals about 12 per cent. of national income. But the total level of 'accumulation' (saving as opposed to consumption) in the national income—including private investments, mainly in agriculture, the amounts set aside for reinvestment in state-private enterprises and subscriptions to Government Savings Bonds—was about 23 per cent. in 1956. This figure probably refers to gross savings, though, as in the Soviet Union, there is no indication of what system of allowance for depreciation, if any, is made. But even for gross savings this is a very high figure indeed; in this respect, too, the Chinese Government's plans seem to be more ambitious than those of the Indian Government, which intends the total level of investment, public and private (excluding foreign aid), under its second Five-Year Plan, to rise to about 10 per cent. of national income by 1962.

The success of the Government's efforts to secure and maintain such a level of saving and investment is likely to be crucial to the accomplishment of their aims in the industrial field. There are, of course, many difficulties in the way of maintaining a high level of investment in any underdeveloped country such as China in the absence of considerable assistance from outside sources. Although China has received substantial aid from the Soviet Union, it seems that all has to be paid for, and that the periods of repayment are indeed fairly short; what is more, this assistance may now be coming to an end. Since the general level of income in underdeveloped countries is not far above subsistence level, the rate of personal saving is very low; this is particularly the case in a country like China today, where there is no wealthier class (as in European countries during the nineteenth century) to provide the savings required. For the same reason the total taxable capacity of such a country is low, and this makes it difficult for the Government too to find the resources to provide a high level of investment. And in China the rapid increase in population will tend even further to reduce taxable capacity among the agricultural population unless means can be found to bring about a marked increase in agricultural production. The rates of taxation which are therefore necessary to provide a sufficient volume of savings in China, both by personal taxation and by the sales tax which in effect is levied through the Government's profits on state enterprises, may have strongly disincentive effects; while on the other hand any increase in purchasing power which may be permitted to offset these effects will be inflationary unless accompanied by an increase in the supply of consumer goods on to the market. But, finally, an increase in consumer goods cannot be brought about without some sacrifice in the level of investment in heavy industry being built up as the basis of the country's economy. There is, therefore, a vicious circle whose origin lies in the basic poverty of the country, that is, in the low level of real income per head of the population.

The Chinese Government appear to have run into the difficulties posed by this cycle in the course of their first Five-Year Plan. They started off by planning for a very high proportion of investment in heavy industry in relation to light industry. Thus, during the early years of the Plan, in order to achieve the maximum possible expansion of heavy industry, only a limited quantity of consumer goods was made available to the population. From the statements made at the time of the wage increase granted in 1956, it appears likely that there was some unrest in labour circles during this time;[1] and there was almost certainly a good deal of dissatisfaction among the peasants

[1] See above, p. 120.

during 1955–6 as a result of the high volume of deliveries demanded by the Government at that period. As a result the Government were apparently obliged to grant a higher general level of income throughout the country. In consequence the Government were also obliged, to prevent inflation, to reduce the proportion of investment in heavy industry to total investment.

The Chinese leaders themselves seem to be conscious of the violent fluctuations which their policies bring about in the pace of development. They sometimes even formulate theories to explain them away. These, as one might expect, tend to derive from the conceptions of the Marxist dialectic, the idea of contradictions finally resolved in a higher synthesis. On 1 April 1960 Li Fu-chun declared, 'the course of development of the national economy is always from imbalance to balance, and from balance to imbalance. Every time this repeats itself it raises production to a higher level, and the national economy advances uninterruptedly by these wave-like movements.' There is no doubt that the idea that the economy will eventually achieve a higher development as a result of a series of sudden surges has exercised some influence on the policies adopted by the Chinese leaders. But at the same time they have always shown a notable readiness to modify policies as soon as serious difficulties manifested themselves. Even the most radical and militant among the leadership have invariably expressed scorn for the 'dogmatists'. They take pride that the thinking of Mao Tse-tung 'combines the universal truths of Marxism-Leninism with the concrete practice of revolution and construction in China'. It is likely, therefore, that the periodic reversals of policy that sometimes take place are related more to a general acceptance that some new stage has now become necessary than to the rise and fall of particular factions among the leadership, as is sometimes suggested.

During the current Five-Year Plan beginning in 1958 the Central Committee of the CCP have proposed that all sections of the population should enjoy an increase in income of about 25–30 per cent. Thus, although the Government may hope to increase the rate of saving among the workers and peasants, they will certainly have to provide a fairly substantial further increase in the supply of consumer goods over the present level during this period. On the other hand it is hoped that the national income as a whole will have increased by 50 per cent. during the same period. The proportion of investment in heavy industry will therefore probably still be substantially higher than that devoted to the consumer-goods industries.

The other main source of investment funds which the Chinese authorities are likely to try to exploit further in the future is the supply of foreign exchange arising from a favourable balance of payments. This is a further incentive to seek to bring about substantial increases in agricultural production. But the increases that can be achieved in this direction will be governed in the long run by the limited area of cultivable land in China. In time, therefore, China's sources of foreign exchange are likely to be acquired more by sales of light industrial products—in which she will become a rival to Japan—than by an agricultural surplus. But it is possible too that the large-scale prospecting that is going on at the moment will reveal further supplies of exportable raw materials, such as the rare metals which already form an important element in Chinese exports.

The next essential requirement which China must fulfil if she is quickly to create a modern industrial economy is to acquire (and to acquire within a much shorter space of time than any of the other great powers have done) an adequate knowledge of modern industrial techniques. The Government has launched a twelve-year plan for scientific and technical development, running parallel to the twelve-year plan for agriculture and other national plans, which will attempt to build up and develop a corpus of basic scientific knowledge, in the field of pure science as well as in the applied branches, to serve as the foundation for the technological development of the future. The Government are also training a large number of scientists and technicians: higher education in China is now principally centred in the scientific subjects.[1]

In order to co-ordinate scientific research, the Government set up early in 1957 a Scientific Planning Commission under the

[1] The Chinese Government claim that by the end of 1957 China had 600,000 'engineers and technicians'; but it is not certain how they define these terms.

State Council. Besides supervising all research in scientific fields, the Commission was to provide for international co-operation in scientific research (an indication of Chinese awareness of the need to learn from other countries), to make arrangements for the training and employment of scientists and technicians, and to welcome back Chinese specialists still in capitalist countries. The specific programmes of research in individual fields are directed by the Planning Committee for Scientific Development. The programme submitted by this body to the State Council for 1956–7 included the study of the peaceful use of atomic energy, radio-electronics, jet-propulsion, automation and precision instruments and the mechanization and electrification of agriculture.

The Chinese appear to be making serious efforts to acquire some knowledge of atomic techniques. In May 1957 it was announced that Chinese scientists expected to complete during 1957 a high-pressure electrostatic accelerator, with an energy capacity of 2·5 million electronic volts. Later in the same month it was announced that an atomic reactor of the heavy-water type with a power output of 7,000 kilowatts, and a 25 million electronic volts cyclotron, was being built in China with Soviet assistance, and would be completed that year. It was said that Chinese scientists could extract pure uranium and thorium from Chinese ores, and that the techniques of radio-active isotopes were being applied in the geological, petroleum, medical, and other fields.

In the task of acquiring a knowledge of modern industrial techniques China is immensely dependent upon the help of the Soviet Union. But, although there is no doubt that the Soviet Union has already been enormously valuable to China in giving assistance in the field of technology, and although there are, or have been, vast numbers (estimates vary between about 10,000 and 50,000) of Soviet technicians in China, helping with the erection of new factories and the installation of modern equipment, it is not certain that the Soviet Union always makes available the very latest and most valuable technical information in all fields. Thus the Chinese are no doubt well aware that in the long run it is essential, if China is to become a first-class industrial power, that they should become completely self-reliant in the field of industrial technology.

The development of a high level of technical knowledge is of special importance for China. Since, as far as is known so far, she is not very rich in raw materials, and her capacity to produce agricultural exports is limited, in the long run her prosperity is likely to depend, like that of the United Kingdom and of Japan, on her ability to make herself into an efficient workshop, relying on a fairly large volume of exports of manufactured goods to pay for her essential imports of materials and, for some time to come, capital equipment. Thus it will be essential that she should be in the front rank in matters of industrial techniques, and the Chinese authorities are likely to continue to devote special attention to the development of 'advanced experience'.

Thirdly, a considerable development of Chinese communications will be necessary. At present the total length of railway in operation (about 20,000 miles) is less than three-fifths of the amount in use in India, and less than a tenth of the length in operation in the United States. There are still huge areas of country where there are no railways at all. It will also be necessary for China to develop production of lorries, at present still a rarity in China, and to build up a fleet of tugs, coasters, and other merchant ships to serve her needs in the field of sea transport. Bottlenecks in communications are still a cause of many difficulties and delays in Chinese industrial production.

Finally, even if all these conditions are fulfilled, no very accurate assessment of China's future as an industrial power can be made without some better knowledge of her endowment of natural resources. Although it is no doubt possible for any country today, through the acquisition of modern techniques, to become and remain an important industrial power, irrespective of its supply of resources, a strong position in this field is obviously of immense value to a developing industrial power. In China's case, it appears on the evidence so far available that supplies of coal and probably of iron are sufficient for her needs for some time to come. Although much has been made of recent discoveries of oil deposits in Sinkiang, Szechwan, and other areas, it is not yet known how far these are economically exploitable. The most that can really be said on present evidence is that China is probably not rich in natural resources, but at the same time not yet so poor that this is likely to be a very serious handicap to her development during the next twenty years or so.

There is of course one resource in which China is extremely rich. That is labour. This is a richness which may well, however, prove an embarrassment rather than an asset. Even at the very fastest rate of expansion which can plausibly be conceived, Chinese industry can be expected to draw off only a negligible proportion of the enormous and ever-growing Chinese population. The Chinese authorities not long ago rebuked industrial enterprises for taking on an additional labour force of 2·5 million people during the course of 1956; this figure was considered double the number of extra workers actually needed. But during that year the total Chinese population, according to the Chinese Minister of Health, increased by 15 million. Thus, even if the agricultural population were to remain stable, a very considerable unemployment problem must inevitably soon arise in the country areas; and in fact the more economic methods that the new co-operative forms of farming were presumably designed to bring about could be expected if anything to reduce the labour force required per unit of land (though a little labour will be taken up in developing new areas). The policy of small-scale industry in the countryside is to some extent a recognition of this difficulty.

In addition, the increases in population are not evenly spaced, but have become progressively larger, especially in the last few years. In about ten years, therefore, the authorities will be faced with a population bulge of the most alarming proportions, and one which, however much they may achieve in the meantime, they are going to have the utmost difficulty in coping with; when it is considered that they will then, within the space of about seven or eight years, have to find employment for about 100 million extra people,[1] some idea of the magnitude of the problem they are facing can be gained.

The population problem is thus crucial for China's economic future. It was no doubt as a result of their recognition of this fact that the authorities have during the last few years gradually

[1] At least temporarily: the Chinese Government may then wish to reconsider their present policy of encouraging married women to work.

relaxed their attitude on the question of birth-control.

The question was broached for the first time in September 1954, about the time when the results of the census were becoming known. Shao Li-tze, a non-Communist, doubtless at the instigation of the authorities, advocated birth-control in the National People's Congress. During 1955–6 there was a good deal more public ventilation of the subject, supplies of appliances were made generally available, and women were encouraged to make use of birth-control methods if there were health reasons making a limitation of births desirable, though it was at first still insisted that there was no danger of over-population in China. Finally, towards the end of 1956, a full-scale campaign for the encouragement of birth-control methods was instituted. The Minister of Health, Mrs. Li Te-chuan, went so far as to say that without such work 'China could not free itself from poverty, and become prosperous, rich ' and strong'. Efforts were to be made to 'break down the traditional opposition to birth-control which was particularly strong in the rural areas'. A sample survey in a Shanghai factory showed that '17 per cent. of the women were pregnant twice in a year [*sic*], 53 per cent. once in a year, and 22 per cent. twice in three years'.

Early in 1957 it was announced that, from March that year, Chinese women would be able to get abortions and sterilization on request. The planned output of contraceptives was increased fivefold and the price reduced 30 to 60 per cent. There were even suggestions for raising the minimum age of marriage (laid down in the Marriage Law as a protection against child marriage) to 23 for men and 20 for women. A revealing indication of the way the campaign may eventually develop was given by a report that the 123 married couples of Kuangming agricul-tural co-operative in Shuanfeng *hsien*, in Hunan Province, had 'decided on planned parenthood, proposing that the birth-rate should decrease from 4 per cent. to 1·8 per cent. within five years'; this presumably is one field in which no bonuses are offered for over-fulfilling production norms.

This campaign was somewhat abated during 1958. It is, in any case, likely to come up against strong opposition. Since in China for many the welfare of the deceased in the next world depends on sacrifices offered by their descendants on earth, the procreation of children and particularly of sons is of special importance. But recent difficulties in agriculture, and the famine conditions resulting, may well cause the Government to revive the programme. A full-scale campaign, backed up by all the propaganda and pressure techniques available to the Government, may prove as successful as the régime's efforts to achieve new culture patterns in other fields, e.g. marriage customs and hygiene.

Parallel with this effort, the Government will sooner or later be obliged to introduce measures to cope, as far as possible, with the large increase in the labour force which is already inevitable. They will no doubt initiate many further large-scale irrigation projects and other public works schemes, even if some of these are not immediately productive, so long as they can absorb at least some of the many millions who, unemployed, might well constitute a dangerous and disruptive social force. They will probably choose methods which give best hope of providing occupation for a larger number of workers, like those recently tried in the Communes. In agriculture they may have to devise methods of increasing, rather than reducing, the labour force used for every unit of cultivable land. In industry they will increasingly be drawn to employ capital-extensive methods in the knowledge that they will probably be able to rely, for a long time to come, on a large supply of labour, which, just because of its size, is likely to remain cheap compared with that employed in other countries.

It is probable that the Chinese economy will continue to develop at an impressive speed. The foundation of heavy industry has already been laid and is now very rapidly expanding. Because of the extremely backward state of the country and the low average standard of living, very large increases in industrial production and substantial improvements in the people's standard of life can be brought about by means of relatively small injections of capital and the application of modern industrial techniques. Similarly, the backward state of agriculture will allow a fairly rapid increase to be made in agricultural production during the first years by the use of more modern methods and equipment, even though there cannot be any very large

increase in the area sown. Although, if the aims of the draft
Plan for the second five-year period are fulfilled, there will be
a considerable rise in the standard of living of both worker and
peasant, on the whole the rapid rate of development will be
achieved, as in other Communist countries, by sacrificing
today's consumer for that of tomorrow. The accomplishment of
these goals, as the Chinese Government have become increasingly aware, is crucially dependent on bringing about a radical
improvement of the agricultural foundation of the economy.
But if the energy and flexibility shown by the authorities in
the economic field so far are maintained, the country's economy
should receive vigorous and intelligent guidance, facilitated by
absolute and unassailable political authority, unchallenged
control of every facet of the economy, and total domination of
all channels of information and opinion.

XVII

CONCLUSIONS

UNTIL recent years the Chinese leaders were probably well satisfied with what they had achieved in the economic field during the period since they came into power. A largely backward economy, with an extremely low volume of capitalization and poor in techniques both in industry and agriculture was transformed, within the space of ten years, into one which was capable of the production of aircraft, lorries, cargo ships, electric generators, locomotives, and automatic lathes. Within this economy a not inconsiderable and rapidly growing sector of modern industry has been built up, a very high rate of investment is being maintained, a knowledge of some of the most modern industrial techniques has been acquired and applied, and more advanced agricultural methods are beginning to be employed. The production of the main industrial commodities has grown several times over the highest previously obtained, and substantial increases brought about in agricultural production. Within the last two years there have been many difficulties and the Chinese world's leaders must accept that China remains among the underdeveloped nations.

During the first three years after their accession to power the Government were largely concerned with achieving as quickly as possible the rehabilitation of the seriously disrupted economy, and with checking the inflationary movement which had played such a large part in bringing about the fall of their predecessors. At the same time they were extending the area of state control within the economy, and acquiring their first experience of the overall direction of its activities. During the early stages of the first Plan there seems to have been a good deal of confusion and inefficiency, due largely to inexperience in planning techniques and to over-ambitious expansion by individual industries and enterprises. During the later stages these mistakes appear to have been to some extent rectified; but in 1956 the rate of expansion achieved over-extended China's resources and serious inflationary pressures made themselves felt. In 1957 the pace was slackened. Nevertheless, the targets of the Five-Year Plan were nearly all passed and in many cases substantially exceeded by the end of that year.

In agriculture there were at first less striking advances. During the first three or four years of the régime there was little increase over the production figures of pre-war days (when there was a considerably smaller agricultural population). Only between 1954 and 1956 was any substantial rise in production achieved. And even by the end of 1957, though agricultural production was probably about 30 per cent. above pre-war levels, production per head was probably little, if any, higher. In 1958 there does appear to have been a very considerable rise. And plans for the future are even more startling. It remains to be seen if these ambitious projects can be realized.

During this time big institutional changes were made. In industry almost all private concerns were by the end of 1956 effectively controlled by the state, while by far the greater part of industry was actually state-owned. During the next two years a substantial proportion of industrial enterprises was handed over to the control of local authorities. In agriculture, between 1949 and the early part of 1958, three major social revolutions took place. Agricultural holdings were first largely equalized by redistribution; they were then amalgamated into larger units under co-operative management; finally these in turn were merged into the still larger communes. By the end of 1958, therefore, the socialization of the Chinese economy had been virtually achieved. Within a few years it would be completed.

From 1958 to 1960, China was carrying out a crash programme designed to achieve the maximum possible results in the shortest possible time. To attain these ends her leaders did not hesitate to call on the Chinese people for three years of sweat and tears. They established small-scale industrial undertakings in the countryside to make the maximum use of the labour force available there. Like their colleagues in the Soviet Union, they transferred the control of some enterprises to local and provincial administrations. The communes were called on to do it themselves by undertaking implement repair, fertilizer production, even, for a time, iron and steel production, to contribute what they can to this effort. At the same time a similar unit of administration in the towns, established only in 1960, was also introduced to play its part by mobilizing manpower in the cities and organizing processing and repair work for the state factories of its area. The aim has been to bring into play every available element among China's still undeveloped resources in order to get rich quick by the shortest possible route.

The Government will no doubt continue to demand the rapid development of heavy industry. Thus, though average consumption will probably rise during the next few years, a considerable proportion of the increase in production attained will be ploughed back into further capital development. But during the next decade it is likely that a great deal more emphasis will be given than during the last to seeking to bring about a substantial rise in agricultural production. As in other underdeveloped countries this is essential not only to raising living standards, but to ensuring economic stability at home and winning the capacity to import the industrial equipment necessary for the future growth of the economy.

A crucial factor will be the growth of the population. Unless some check can be put upon this, the Government will have great difficulty in bringing about any substantial rise in the standard of living of the people. Indeed, they are likely to have great difficulty in absorbing the increases which have already occurred.

The present administration has shown itself able and ambitious in its direction of the economy. In its eyes the need for a powerful Chinese economy is a political, almost as much as an economic one. This is required not only to improve the standard of living of the Chinese people, but to increase China's power and prestige, and so her influence among her neighbours. On 1 October 1957 Liu Shao-chi called on the Chinese people to develop their tradition of hard work and thrift 'in order to build China into the richest and most powerful country in the world'. Few would dare to assert that this aim will not be achieved.

Up to the present China's progress in industrialization has been largely dependent on the help of the Soviet Union. This has implications which are political as well as economic. It is possible that in future China will have increasing difficulty in obtaining from this source supplies of capital or equipment on the scale she would like. She may therefore be increasingly driven to seek other sources of aid. Certainly it is likely that in future, especially with the further growth of a modern and self-supporting industrial economy, sustained by the massive weight of her enormous population, China will speak with increasing independence in her dealings with the Soviet Union.

The prospects for the future development of the Chinese economy depend largely on the successful limitation of the population's growth, on the capacity of the Chinese to acquire and develop modern industrial techniques, and on the success of the Government in holding in check the demands of the consumer while the capital resources of the country are being built up. There can, however, already be little doubt that the industry and intelligence of the Chinese people, together with the overwhelming weight of their numbers, are likely to create in the Chinese economy a force that will have a rapidly increasing impact on the world in the years to come.

STATISTICAL APPENDIX

Note: The source for all figures is the Chinese State Statistical Bureau. The form in which Chinese statistics appear underwent a change during 1956. It is not therefore possible to provide all the relevant figures for the later years.

1. Output of Leading Industrial Products in China

	Unit	Pre-Communist Peak Year		1949	1952	1953	1954	1955	1956	1957	1958	1959
		Year	Output									
Coal	'000 tons	1942	61,875	30,984	63,528	66,572	79,928	93,064	105,922	124,180	270,000	347,800
Power	m. kwh.	1941	5,955	4,308	7,261	9,195	11,001	12,278	16,590	19,010	27,500	41,500
Crude oil	'000 tons	1943	320	122	436	622	789	966	1,163	1,420	2,230	3,700
Pig-iron	"	1943	1,801	246	1,900	2,175	2,962	3,630	4,777	5,860	..	..
Steel	"	1943	923	158	1,349	1,774	2,225	2,853	4,465	5,240	8,000	13,350
Sulphate of ammonia	"	1941	227	27	181	226	298	324	..	740*	..	..
Cement	"	1942	2,293	661	2,861	3,877	4,600	4,502	6,393	6,690	..	12,270
Metal-cutting machines	units	1941	5,390	1,582	13,734	20,502	15,901	13,708	26,000	29,100	90,000	70,000
Cotton yarn	'000 bales	1933	2,447	1,803	3,618	4,104	4,598	3,968	5,246	4,650	6,660	..
Cotton cloth	'000 bolts	1936	45,008	30,178	89,273	107,794	122,331	103,220	4,600†	5,050†	6,404†	7,500†
Motor tyres	units	1943	75,000	26,020	417,184	488,067	701,259	593,241				
Paper	'000 tons	1943	165	108	372	427	556	589	746	906	..	1,700
Sugar	"				249	298	347	410	518	558	..	..
Cigarettes	'000 cases	1947	2,363	1,600	2,650	3,552	3,728	3,567	3,907	4,317	..	..

Note: Production in this table does not include that of handicrafts. Paper includes cardboard.
* Chemical fertilizer.   † m. metres cotton piece goods.

2. Value of Industrial Production in China
(million yuan, expressed in 1952 fixed prices[1])

	1949	1952	1953	1954	1955	1956	1957
TOTAL PRODUCTION	10,781	27,014	35,577	41,513	44,748	58,620	62,810
Of which:							
Capital goods	3,100	10,730	14,670	17,578	20,578	29,100	..
Consumer goods	7,681	16,284	20,907	23,935	24,170	29,520	..
Incl. in total:							
Machine-building ind.	188	1,401	2,157	2,645	3,030	..	..
Of the total:							
State-operated	3,683	14,258	19,239	24,488	28,142	31,950	..
Co-operative-operated	50	863	1,216	1,598	2,152	10,030	..
Joint state-private	220	1,367	2,013	5,086	7,188	15,880	..
Privately operated	6,828	10,526	13,109	10,341	7,266	760	..

Note: This table does not include production of handicraft co-operatives and individual handicraftsmen.

3. Production of Major Agricultural Crops in China
('000 tons)

	1949	1952	1953	1954	1955	1956	1957	1958	1959
Grains	113,181	163,913	166,832	169,513	183,993	192,716	185,000*	250,000*	270,000*
Of which:									
Rice	48,645	68,426	71,272	70,851	78,024	...	...	...	...
Wheat	13,808	18,123	18,281	23,332	22,965	...	...	...	...
Miscellaneous grains	35,799	51,519	50,695	49,269	54,926	...	...	...	...
Potatoes (incl. sweet potatoes)	9,843	16,326	16,653	16,981	18,897	...	...	...	...
Soya beans	5,086	9,519	9,931	9,080	9,121	10,250	...	...	...
Cotton	444	1,304	1,175	1,065	1,518	1,445	1,640	2,100	2,410
Jute and kenafe	37	305	138	137	257	257	...	...	...
Flue-cured tobacco	43	222	213	232	298	399	...	...	...
Sugar-cane	2,642	7,116	7,209	8,592	8,110	8,678	...	...	...
Sugar beets	191	479	505	989	1,596	1,644	...	...	...
Peanuts	1,268	2,316	2,127	2,767	2,926	3,326	...	...	...
Rapeseed	734	932	879	878	969	921	...	...	...

* Excluding soya beans.

4. Capital Investment in Different Sectors of the Chinese Economy, 1952–5

(million yuan)

	Absolute Figures				Percentage of Total			
	1952	1953	1954	1955	1952	1953	1954	1955
TOTAL INVESTMENTS	3,711	6,506	7,498	8,212	100·0	100·0	100·0	100·0
of which:								
Industry	1,549	2,756	3,634	4,204	41·7	42·4	48·5	51·2
Building	92	345	355	290	2·5	5·3	4·7	3·5
Agriculture	186	276	144	199	5·0	4·2	1·9	2·4
Water conservancy	331	376	219	402	8·9	5·8	2·9	4·9
Railways	502	642	917	1,202	13·5	9·9	12·2	14·6
Communications	229	354	445	452	6·2	5·4	5·9	5·5
Culture, education, and health	320	767	771	689	8·6	11·8	10·3	8·4
City construction	171	250	232	218	4·6	3·8	3·1	2·7
Other	331	740	781	556	9·0	9·4	10·5	6·8

Note: The actual investments made in 1955 amounted to 8,630 million yuan; the figures listed include only those items which can be compared with figures of previous years.

The values listed are based on the estimated prices for the relevant years. According to the Chinese authorities, as a result of the reduction of building costs and prices of equipment, the figures do not represent fully the rate of increase of the actual volume of work carried out.

5. Livestock Population
('000 head)

	1949	1952	1953	1954	1955	1956
Cattle	43,936	56,600	60,083	63,623	65,951	66,611
Horses	4,875	6,130	6,512	6,939	7,312	7,385
Donkeys	9,494	11,806	12,215	12,700	12,402	11,656
Mules	1,471	1,637	1,645	1,717	1,723	1,706
Sheep & goats	42,347	61,779	72,023	81,304	84,218	..
Pigs	57,752	89,765	96,131	101,718	87,920	84,403

6. Development of Agricultural Mutual Aid and Co-operation
('000 households)

							Percentage of Participants of all Peasant Households					
	1950	1952	1953	1954	1955	1956	1950	1952	1953	1954	1955	1956
Total peasant households	105,536	113,683	116,331	117,331	119,201	125,000	100·0	100·0	100·0	100·0	100·0	100·0
Total participant households in mutual aid and co-operation	11,313	45,423	45,912	70,775	77,310	120,000	10·7	40·0	39·5	60·3	64·9	96·0
Agricultural co-operatives	0·219	59	275	2,297	16,921	120,000	..	0·1	0·2	2·0	14·2	96·0
Of which:												
Higher co-operatives	0·032	1·8	2·1	12	40	100,000	..	..	..	..	..	88·0
Lower co-operatives	0·187	57	273	2,285	16,881	20,000	..	..	0·2	1·9	14·2	8·0
Mutual-aid teams	11,313	45,364	45,637	68,478	60,389	..	10·7	39·9	39·3	58·4	50·7	..
Of which:												
Permanent teams	..	11,448	13,329	30,713	32,843	..	..	10·1	11·5	26·2	27·6	..
Seasonal teams	..	33,916	32,308	37,765	27,546	..	..	29·8	27·8	32·2	23·1	..

Note: Figures for Mutual Aid and Co-operation refer to those actually participating in production in the year, and sharing in the distribution of autumn harvest.

Farms under Ministry of Agriculture

	Unit	1950	1952	1953	1954	1955	1956
No. of state farms	one	1,215	2,336	2,376	2,415	2,242	450
Cultivated acreage	'000 hectares	155·0	246·9	250·8	294·5	394·6	900
No. of mechanized farms	one	36	50	59	97	106	166
Cultivated acreage	'000 hectares	89·3	135·8	141·3	185·8	269·3	448·0

7. Value of Public and Private Retail Sales of Commodities
(million yuan)

	1950	1952	1953	1954	1955	1956	Percentages of Total					
							1950	1952	1953	1954	1955	1956
TOTAL	16,794	27,665	35,041	38,962	40,002	..	100·0	100·0	100·0	100·0	100·0	100·0
State economy	1,331	4,384	5,941	7,611	10,785	..	7·9	15·8	17·0	·19·5	27·0	68·0
Co-operative economy	819	5,051	8,519	14,901	12,211	..	4·9	18·3	24·3	38·3	30·5	12·0
State-capitalist economy	31	77	152	1,827	5,065	..	0·2	0·3	0·4	4·7	12·7	17·0
Private economy (incl. peasant trading)	14,613	18,153	20,429	14,623	11,941	..	87·0	65·6	58·3	37·5	29·8	3·0

SELECT BIBLIOGRAPHY

Adler, Solomon. *The Chinese Economy*. New York, Monthly Review Press, 1957.

Buck, J. L. *Land Utilization in China*. Nanking University, 1937.

East, W. G. and O. K. Spate. *The Changing Map of Asia*. London, Methuen, 1950.

Fei, Hsiao-tung. *Peasant Life in China*. London, Routledge, 1939.

Gluckstein, Ygael. *Mao's China*. Boston, Beacon Press, 1957.

Moraes, F. R. *Report on Mao's China*. New York, Macmillan, 1953.

Rostow, W. W. and others. *The Prospects for Communist China*. Cambridge, Mass., Inst. of Technology, 1954.

Shabad, T. *China's Changing Map*. New York, Praeger, 1956.

Snow, Edgar. *Red Star over China*. London, Gollancz, 1937.

Tawney, R. H. *Land and Labour in China*. London, Allen, 1932.

Thomas, S. B. *Government and Administration in Communist China*. 2nd ed. New York, Inst. of Pacific Relations, 1955.

Wu, Yuan-li. *An Economic Survey of Communist China*. New York, Bookman Associates, 1956.

INDEX